PRAISE FOR KRIS CARR

Kris Carr's riveting journey started a revolution. She's irreverent and she's aggressive and she's vulnerable and she's an absolute game changer.
— **Oprah Winfrey**

Kris Carr is a beacon of light. Her message should inspire us all to take hold of our lives.
— **Dr. Mark Hyman**

Kris is the ray of light that is needed to raise awareness. She is a true leader of courage and inspiration.
— **Donna Karan**

My friend Kris Carr is brilliant and inspiring.
— **Sheryl Crow**

Friends: I recommend Kris Carr's work. It will enhance your well-being.
— **Deepak Chopra**

I'm Not a Mourning Person

ALSO BY KRIS CARR

Crazy Sexy Cancer Tips

*Crazy Sexy Cancer Survivor: More Rebellion
and Fire for Your Healing Journey*

*Crazy Sexy Diet: Eat Your Veggies, Ignite Your Spark,
and Live Like You Mean It!*

*Crazy Sexy Juice: 100+ Simple Juice, Smoothie & Nut Milk
Recipes to Supercharge Your Health**

*Crazy Sexy Kitchen: 150 Plant-Empowered Recipes to
Ignite a Mouthwatering Revolution (with Chad Sarno)**

Crazy Sexy Love Notes (card deck)*

The Results Journal

*Available from Hay House
Please visit:

Hay House USA: www.hayhouse.com®
Hay House Australia: www.hayhouse.com.au
Hay House UK: www.hayhouse.co.uk
Hay House India: www.hayhouse.co.in

***

I'm Not a Mourning Person

BRAVING LOSS, GRIEF, AND THE
BIG MESSY EMOTIONS THAT HAPPEN
WHEN LIFE FALLS APART

KRIS CARR

HAY HOUSE, INC.
Carlsbad, California • New York City
London • Sydney • New Delhi

Published in the United States by: Hay House, Inc.: www.hayhouse.com®
Published in Australia by: Hay House Australia Pty. Ltd.: www.hayhouse.com.au
Published in the United Kingdom by: Hay House UK, Ltd.: www.hayhouse.co.uk
Published in India by: Hay House Publishers India: www.hayhouse.co.in

Cover design: Pete Graceau
Interior design: Karim J. Garcia

Cataloging-in-Publication Data is on file at the Library of Congress

Hardcover ISBN: 978-1-4019-7006-2
E-book ISBN: 978-1-4019-7007-9
Audiobook ISBN: 978-1-4019-7008-6

10 9 8 7 6 5 4 3 2
1st edition, September 2023

Printed in the United States of America

SUSTAINABLE FORESTRY INITIATIVE

Certified Chain of Custody
Promoting Sustainable Forestry
www.forests.org
SFI-01268

SFI label applies to the text stock

This product uses paper and materials from responsibly sourced forests. For more information, please go to: bookchainproject.com/home.

For Dad

CONTENTS

INTRODUCTION

Never Let Them See You Grieve

Only cry in the shower. No one will see you, and you won't wreck your mascara.

This bit of wisdom was given to me by a family friend when my father was dying.

At the time, overwhelmed by emotion and desperately trying to maintain some semblance of control, I thought it was a brilliant tip. Not only did I attempt to follow this guideline—I also added a few of my own. Things like: *Stuff yourself into the nearest closet and scream into a pillow (or any dense fabric that muffles agony). Dig your nails into your palms so the physical pain overrides your emotional distress. Think gruesome thoughts to distract yourself from your grueling feelings.* These strategies worked for a while, until my pent-up sorrow took on a life of its own, refusing to abide by any rules.

I remember the exact moment the dam broke. My dad had just received news that his cancer was progressing and there were no more treatment options. Numb from the arresting prognosis, I walked through the aisles of my local drugstore, having offered to run an errand to pick up more Ensure—the only nourishment he could stomach. I stood frozen, staring at the chocolate-flavored protein drinks, incapable of deciding how many to buy. *Will he live long enough for a case, or should I just stick to the four-packs?*

That question hit me hard. An emotional tsunami was about to unleash itself on me and all the innocent shoppers in my immediate vicinity.

Shit! Here come my feelings. And no shower in sight. I blinked heavily through the checkout line, fighting back the deluge of tears that were mere seconds away, until I was able to rush to the safety of my car and sob uncontrollably. Let me tell you: the parking lot at CVS is no shower stall. My once-compartmentalized grief was now on full display. Hunched over my steering wheel in a teary puddle, I happened to notice an older woman, probably coming to fetch a prescription or buy toilet paper, glancing my way. She could plainly see what I'd been so desperate to hide: I was a full-blown mess.

After the remains of my mascara finished streaming down my face, I felt a sense of relief similar to when medicine kicks in, giving you a break from a hallucinogenic fever. I'd somehow overlooked how cleansing it could be to let my feelings rip. After this happened a few more times (shout-out to Home Depot and their decision to pipe Michael Bolton's "How Am I Supposed to Live Without You?" through their stereo system), I'd started to realize that these breaks helped me survive. They made me realize that the only way through my sadness was to allow the waves of big feelings to move through my body—something I'd been hell-bent on avoiding, for fear I would drown.

If embracing my intense emotions helped me feel even the slightest bit better, why had I been so determined to avoid them? And given how all-encompassing these hints of catharsis felt, I couldn't help but wonder, *Where else in my life have I been avoiding grief?* Did that avoidance have anything to do with the strange existential angst that had been creeping up on me over the last few years, where I sensed that I was not, in fact, living as fully as I could be?

The more I thought about it, the instinct to avoid grief made perfect sense to me. As well-meaning as my family friend's advice was, *Keep that mascara intact, honey* was not going to help me heed my soul's call to grow. For that, I would need to surrender to my grief and other big emotions.

GIVE YOURSELF PERMISSION TO FEEL

While we may not want to even *think* about grief, loss, or unexpected (and unwanted) change, in order to feel less alone, less broken, less crazy (you're not!), we need to talk about *and* tend to our most tender feelings. We also need to find the right kind of support for our emotions and ourselves in the process. Only then will we be able to pick up the pieces of our shattered hearts and lives and put ourselves back together. Only then can we heal. That is what this book is all about: learning how to be a Mourning Person when we'd rather stay under the covers and go back to sleep.

That said, I'm not going to sugarcoat it: grief sucks—and it isn't a solo flier. Grief rolls with an entourage of complicated friends, who all demand bottle service at the club—emotions like weariness, judgment, shame, jealousy, self-loathing, and all the other not-so-glamorous feelings we don't want people to know we're experiencing.

This is to be expected, and so is the lengthy amount of time it takes to feel like a human being who wants to get out of pajamas as a complete wardrobe and wash her hair again. That's because grief isn't linear. It will work us over in whatever way it wants, and on its own damn schedule. We can't just snap our fingers and be done with the devastation. We also can't amputate any of our emotions and expect to be whole. Believe me, I've tried.

For most of my life, I've done everything in my power to run from the big, scary feelings explored in this book—the socially unacceptable emotions that we're not "supposed" to feel, like rage, powerlessness, and utter despair. But a few years ago, when my father was dying, my world was falling apart, and I was on the verge of reaching my 20-year milestone of living with my own shit pickle—a stage IV cancer diagnosis (yup, it's not gone, neat, or tidy)—I suddenly lost the energy to run. So I decided to try something different: I stopped and faced my feelings.

Eager to find a framework that resonated, I began researching how grief and other difficult emotions affect our brains, bodies, and lives—even when we're unaware of it. Could understanding these big kahunas help me understand myself and others better? Could accepting grief as a part of me that needed to be cared for—just like my skin or heart or the dozens of tumors that I've learned to coexist with—help me feel even the slightest bit whole again? I didn't know, but I needed to try.

So, I slowly and gently started applying the practices, insights, and therapies I was discovering to my own pain, and over time, I eventually began to feel better—not cured, but better. Which is exactly what can happen for you.

Let's be honest: feelings are slippery little suckers. When we deny them, they get pissed off and come out in other, more destructive ways. Uncared for pain can morph into anger, violence, addiction, anxiety, hypervigilance, hyperdrive, guilt, procrastination, hopelessness, and, of course, the consuming of copious amounts of wine. It shrinks our worlds and makes us feel stuck—at home, at work, in our bodies, in our relationships, and in our hearts.

Burying pain can also make us sick or, at the very least, constipated.

But here's what can happen when we're brave enough to take care of our hearts: our messy emotions can teach us how to be free—not free from pain but free from the *fear* of pain and the barrier it creates to fully living.

As trauma specialist Robert Stolorow points out, our feelings, no matter what they are, long for a home. Creating that home, a place where all parts of us are welcome, is how we heal. Grief, loss, and pain beg for a safe place to be seen and heard. They ask us to be vulnerable, which is the last thing we want to do when we're in agony. But if we're brave enough to let our various griefs do their therapeutic work, they will grow and mend us in ways we can't begin to imagine (yet).

And when it comes to healing, there's a bigger picture at play. Humans are interconnected beings, different but bound by our shared experience of being alive. As such, our healing can have a ripple effect on others, too. As we forgive, and unlock and release our pain, we create an opening for others to do the same. But it doesn't stop there. Our healing even has the power to contribute to the healing of ancestral wounds carried down the genetic line. Yet another reason this work is so important.

Grief cracks you open and teaches you priceless, heart-expanding, and healing lessons, too. It certainly has done that for me. It can be used as a catalyst to take inventory of your life, figure out what matters most versus what you can let go of, and allow you to reset, breathing into the next phase of brave, courageous, and utterly unique *you*.

YOU ARE NOT ALONE

Since the onset of the pandemic, the grief, shock, depression, and trauma of the last few years have been astounding. For many of us, this disorientation has prompted some deep soul-searching. Everywhere people are reassessing their values and priorities as a result of losses that will affect us for generations to come.

Because of what we've all been through, we may be more likely to consider the person we walk by in the grocery store, who, like us, might be quietly carrying the burden of their own pain. Loss is the one thing we *all* have in common.

We'll get dumped or do the dumping, we'll quit or get fired, we'll lose our connection to self and wonder why we're here in the first place, and we'll get sick and better and sick again. Our hearts will shatter and swell with fullness. And our resilience is the only thing that allows us to be brave enough to continue loving.

Our mere existence requires us to strengthen our heart muscle through the back-and-forth of love and loss—two experiences that may feel like polar opposites but are actually two sides of the same coin. You can't have one without the other.

The kind of love I'm talking about here is messy and honest. It guides us when we have the courage to follow it. It asks us to do very beautiful and difficult things, like stand up for someone else, or ourselves, or choose what feels right instead of what looks good.

The fierceness of this love invites us to heal old wounds that keep playing out in our day-to-day lives. And most of all, it reminds us that mortality is its price of admission. This kind of love never dies, even when chapters in our lives close or relationships end.

Now, if someone had said this stuff to me before my dad died, I might have wanted to believe it, while also thinking, *Suuuure*. So, if you're having a similar response, I get it. But please hear me out. Putting love at the center of our lives helps us manage our grief and move forward—not "move on" but move *forward*. Not forgetting the person, job, or relationship, but learning how to live without them.

While life will never be the same after whatever loss you're grappling with, it's still worth putting yourself out there and living and loving *fully*. Not because your person "would want you to" (while likely true, no one wants to hear that) and not because "God doesn't give you more than you can handle" (seriously, WTF?), but because life is beautiful. And you deserve to bask in that beauty before your own eventual dirt nap—which can sneak up on you real fast—so you might as well get busy living.

LEARNING AND LIVING THROUGH OUR STORIES

Surrendering to our big messy feelings makes us vulnerable, so the following pages naturally contain many of my embarrassing, painful, helpful, hilarious, and inappropriate stories and observations from the trenches of love and loss. If you've ever freaked out in a random parking lot, you are not alone.

Just as my story is my medicine, so, too, is yours. And while you may see parts of yourself in my journey, you won't find a specific blueprint here. That's because this journey is unique and deeply personal. There is no universal map, but there are common themes, emotional experiences, and useful ideas we'll explore together.

I've also interwoven helpful practices throughout. In some chapters I include a "Caring for . . ." section with additional tips and tools at the end of the chapter. In others, the bulk of the guidance is woven into the narrative. Either way, this book is filled with research and recommendations on what to expect when you're not expecting your world to fall apart.

With more and more evidence connecting the dots between our emotional and physical health, it's increasingly clear how important it is to do this work.

My hope is that this book can be a source of comfort for anyone suffering from a loss—whether it be the dissolving of a relationship or marriage, the end of a job or career, or any number of other significant unexpected transitions. But especially for those wrestling with that pain that comes from an illness or the death of a loved one.

All that said, I hate that we have to do this. I'd much rather watch our favorite Netflix series or make paninis or go shopping for new throw pillows, but here we are. The truth is, you wouldn't be holding this book (and I wouldn't have written it) if life didn't kick us in the choppers. We'd be on a beach somewhere sipping a colada. And we'll likely do that again, but first, we've got some heart-tending to do together.

So, I invite you to be my co-pilot on this healing trip as we tour some of the most difficult and treasured parts of life: grieving and loving, stumbling and flying, living and dying. I'll bring the snacks, flashlights, and bandages. You bring the sensible shoes.

Ready? Let's go.

I'm Not OK

Our pain carves out a larger space for love to fill.

— KHALIL GIBRAN

Days before my dad "got on the bus"—his euphemism for dying—I peeked into his bedroom. Did he need another blanket or some ice chips? Were the lights too bright? Was there anything I could do to make him more comfortable?

That's when I overheard him steadying and calming himself with a mantra. His voice was reduced to a raspy, faint whisper, but his words held the power to stick with me forever.

"It will be OK. I will be OK. It will be OK."

Eyes closed. Hands gently folded on his heart. Deep breaths.

"It will be OK. I will be OK. It will be OK."

Witnessing him trying to comfort himself stopped me in my tracks. Dad had spent his entire life making sure everyone else was OK. Did you need a little extra pocket money? A ride somewhere? A shoulder to cry on or a few wise words to help you make an important decision? He was the go-to guy. I'd seen his caregiver instincts in action with so many of our family and friends. In the awkward or painful moments of life, he was *that* guy, the one unafraid to pull someone aside and say, "What's doin'? You OK?"

A nurturer to many, here he was, in the twilight of his life, nurturing himself. It's hard to explain the swell of emotions I felt—pride (*My dad is amazing!*), heartache (*How could our time together have come to this?*), and genuine appreciation (he was a teacher until the very end—and beyond). I've since learned that it's not uncommon to witness the powerful instincts that take over when people are knocking on heaven's door. The human spirit knows what to do. I was humbled to witness this in Dad.

My father was in the hospice phase of his battle with stage IV pancreatic cancer. His final wish was to die at home, which my mom and I, with steadfast support from my husband, Brian, had worked to honor, arranging for hospice nurses, medical equipment and support, and meal trains. Surrounded by family and his beloved dogs, Jack and Ella, his final days were full of life-on-pause moments like this one, deeply serene and sacred.

Until the jackhammers kicked in. Literally.

When I ripped open the curtains, I saw an entire wrecking crew tearing up a concrete pool in my parents' neighbor's backyard.

Are you fucking kidding me?

As far as I was concerned, Dad could go any minute now. His nurses had basically said as much, alerting us to "expect the unexpected," which is something we were already growing used to. His once-flush complexion was now a constant state of pale. His previously athletic body had withered down to nearly half his regular body weight.

Seemingly overnight, he'd started retaining fluid in his abdomen, something the lean golfer in him would have hated in "normal" times. For the physical changes alone, death by cancer can be a mindfuck. Patients can go from "bad" to "actively dying" in the blink of an eye. Whatever happened, I was not about to let him leave this planet listening to the earsplitting sounds of a piston hitting a striker plate up to 1,800 times per minute.

If you've ever watched as a loved one gets ready to leave this world, you can understand the ferocious mama bear instincts that instantly took over me. *Dad does not need construction right now. He needs Enya!* (Or maybe *I* needed Enya.)

His pain had risen to levels that required round-the-clock morphine. Though I couldn't experience his physical agony firsthand, his pain sure felt like my pain every time I heard him groan. In the coming days, he would no longer be able to communicate with us. His language would go from a few words to hand squeezes to nothing. Step-by-step, he walked closer to his transition. I watched helplessly as Dad straddled an unfamiliar divide between holding on and completely letting go of control.

For me, being in control has always been like wrapping myself in a warm, safe woobie. I dress-rehearse worst-case scenarios all the time, just to make sure that I'm never caught off guard. Yeah, I'm *that* person.

But you know what totally ambushed me as Dad's days started to dwindle? How there was absolutely nothing I could do to protect him. No amount of wishful thinking (*If I never drop f-bombs again, maybe Dad will suddenly get better*) or desperate prayer (*Dude, can we work with the timeline here?*) would help me stop his organs from slowly shutting down, right before my eyes.

What I could control, though, was putting an immediate stop to the thunderous mechanical appliances shaking our house and messing up our hospice zen.

Twenty seconds later, I was marching past the "Danger. No Trespassing" sign on the neighbor's lawn and approaching the crew of dust-covered construction workers.

"Excuse me? Excuuuse me! Hi. Hello there!" I shouted to no one in particular. "Could you please stop *jackhammering*? My dad is dying in the house next door. He doesn't have much time left, and I need you to help me make sure that a *jackhammer* isn't the last sound he hears."

"Uh . . ." They looked at each other with a mixture of confusion and disbelief, before a brawny dude with a gentle soul softly said, "You bet, ma'am. Sorry."

Then there was quiet. Ahhh . . .

"May God bless you, fellas!" I yelled on my way out.

Where that came from, I'm not sure, because I'm a part-time atheist—mostly on Sundays. Yet as the saying goes, there are no atheists in foxholes, and boy did I need God in that moment (or someone like her).

The soundtrack of jackhammers may have subsided, but inside, my adrenaline was still totally jacked. I couldn't stop thinking about what was *actually* going to happen as Dad came closer to the threshold, passing from this glorious and sometimes stress-inducing life to mysterious death. Where was he going? What would life even be without Dad's beaming smile and familiar "Hi, love. What's doin'?" And how the heck was I going to live in the world without this person who played such an important and valuable role in my life?

ANTICIPATORY GRIEF

With each urgent question came another surge of cortisol and anticipatory grief, which I didn't know was a thing until I was going through entire tissue boxes in my downtime, even though Dad was still very much alive at that point.

I've since learned that grief doesn't just magically appear after loss, like sudden-onset diarrhea might come on after too much onion dip. Instead, it often begins long before life ends.

Anticipatory grief is especially common for patients living with terminal illness, as well as for their caregivers. But because this surreal in-between stage is so foreign, it's easy to feel like you're doing something wrong, or like you can't let the person who is sick see your worry, so you have to keep your feelings to yourself.

Old ideas about grief, coupled with a general lack of awareness around anticipatory grief, can further muddy the waters and make us feel more alone. A friend of mine had this experience when she reached out to a therapist, asking if she could join the therapist's grief support group, only to learn that since her near-death loved one was still technically alive, the therapist wouldn't invite her to the group. "Call me when she dies." Really?

However anticipatory grief is handled, not to mention received, there's a strong notion that it's better to keep these "downer" feelings to ourselves. Of course, just the opposite is true.

In my case, anticipatory grief began several years before my dad died, the very first moment I realized that his health was in major peril. I found myself hyperfocused on every doctor's appointment and spent many a night weeping into my pasta bowl as I got lost in fantasies about how his absence might feel. No more summer birthday celebrations (his and mine). No more calls to talk about what just happened on our favorite TV series. No more Dad. When I first started experiencing this kind of grief, I freaked out. What if all my future-tripping about life without him was putting bad energy out into the universe and jinxing his survival chances? These superstitious thoughts only made me fear my feelings even more.

Anticipatory grief also triggers the same raw, unpredictable emotions that come with loss. Fear, sadness, anger, betrayal, shame, anger, loneliness, denial, hopelessness . . . did I mention anger? Just wanted to be sure.

I should note that anticipatory grief doesn't happen for everyone, and that's OK, too. Some people may have an easier time staying in the present moment. Or simply don't go there because . . . they *don't* go there. No judgment either way.

Anticipatory grief also doesn't replace or resolve the grief we experience after loss. It doesn't even make it easier. It's just another normal part of a painful journey that calls to be honored. Apparently, grief doesn't like to be neatly tucked into a box, either. At least we have that in common.

LETTING GO OF CONTROL

After years of us aggressively advocating on Dad's behalf—could there be another doctor, trial, or integrative therapy we could try?—his doctor had called for no more treatment. I finally had to recognize (bitterly, I might add) that the only thing left to do was to make Dad feel as comfortable as possible in the time he had left. As I once heard grief expert David Kessler say, "There's a time to fight, and there's a time to ride the damn horse in the direction it's going."

Dad was saddling up, and our final job was to help him prepare for his journey. To strap ourselves to the unbearable present moment. But on any given day, I was oscillating between three modes: fight, flight, or WTF!? How the hell was I going to show up fully for this human I loved so dearly, when I was in a perpetual state of panic?

Dad seemed to have an easier time with this shift to comfort care, like he had seen this moment coming. I never saw any outbursts or breakdowns, just a quiet, graceful transition to his transition. But while he was making peace with death and with himself, I was fighting like a hooked marlin. I didn't want to let go of control because on some level, I believed that control was the only thing keeping him here and us all together. Letting go felt like letting him down—which I now know wasn't true but at the time felt very real.

But my need for control, and the pain it was causing me, kept me from staying present and experiencing the moments that mattered. Though I was terrified of what was to come, I was even more scared of having regrets later. I wanted Dad to feel every ounce of my love until his last breath. So for better or worse, I had to try to accept what was happening—even though I didn't want to and wasn't ready for it.

Fighting reality, which includes pain, was only causing more suffering (which is hard to see when you're in the vortex of loss). Surrendering to reality was clearly the way forward, but to do so I had to remember the medicine inherent in that action. Many of us equate surrender or acceptance with quitting or giving up, but I've come to learn that through the power of surrender we're able to lay down the stress, anxiety, and heavy burdens that keep us running in the opposite direction of love.

In the end, Dad didn't just make peace with death, he made peace with himself, and in the process, he showed me a majestic picture window of what's possible in my own life. Death and mortality will do that—reveal a hidden guide for life and healing. No matter how ferocious life can be, there's always a way back home to ourselves, the safe place where we can find peace and be calmed by the presence of love.

This may sound weird, but the more Dad did this work on himself, the more he started to literally shine. It wasn't just the natural changes in the pallor of his skin as he got closer to the end; it was that he was filled with light, emanating a radiance that truly felt otherworldly. If we were strangers at a bar, I might have seen his glow and said to the bartender: "I'll have whatever that guy's having." But we were not strangers. He was, in so many ways, my person.

TOM SELLECK MUSTACHE

While Dad wasn't my biological father, he was my rock, and I was his "sweet pea." Essential to our father-daughter bond was this simple fact: we chose each other.

I met him when I was nine years old, at my maternal grandfather's funeral. My mother and I were walking toward the front of the church when this tall man with a slightly receding hairline stood up and gave her a kiss on the cheek.

My mother blushed. She was smitten, clearly. Which made hypervigilant me very suspicious. *Who the heck is this dude?* I thought. Up until then, it had always been me, my mom, and my grandma. Three generations of fiery women, all under one broken roof.

I fancied myself the top dog in the family, so while the rest of the people sang hymns and mourned my dear grandpa's passing, I gave Ken my best stink eye. He didn't even blink. Apparently, I wasn't as scary as I'd hoped. In fact, the more I cast darts his way, the more he struggled to contain a smile.

My suspicion escalated to full-blown horror the first night he slept over. We'd just finished dinner when my mom excused herself to her room. *What is going on?* I wondered. *I don't want to hang out with this guy!* I swiftly stomped up the stairs and found her changing her sheets.

"What are you doing?" I demanded. "You have a *guest* downstairs. Now is not the time to do chores."

Despite the fact that I hadn't even reached the height requirement to ride a roller coaster, I sincerely believed that I could—and frankly, should—call the shots. Mom, who had a string of questionable Romeos in her rearview, wasn't always the best judge of character. Not that she saw it that way. Familiar with my bossy-boots tendencies, Mom didn't even glance up as she replied matter-of-factly, "Ken is staying over."

No one had *ever* stayed over. My head exploded. I didn't have words—not ones I could say out loud without being sent to my room, anyway. I ran downstairs, got a piece of paper, and penned a letter to the stranger in my midst:

> *Dear Ken,*
> *You are not my father.*
> *And I do not like your mustache.*
> *Are we clear?*

(In his defense, facial hair was all the rage in the '80s, when Tom Selleck—heartthrob of *Magnum, P.I.* and the

"Sexiest Man Alive"—had set the gold standard of rugged masculinity with his thick, dark mustache.)

Thankfully, my mother intercepted the letter. I say "thankfully," because as scared as I had been about losing whatever modicum of third-grade "control" I had over my household, I ultimately imprinted on Ken like a little duckling—hatched from her defensive, hardscrabble shell—and immediately attached to him. In no time, that attachment blossomed into deep admiration, trust, and unconditional love.

For all my scrappiness, what I had always wanted most was a dad. A real dad. A present dad, like my classmates' dads, who came to after-school sports, glowed at parent-teacher conferences, and rewarded good grades with hot fudge sundaes. Not only had I never met my biological father, I didn't even know his name, never mind any details about his identity. My mother avoided the topic, and my very dramatic grandmother offered conflicting stories. *Your father died in a plane crash.* (He didn't.) *Your parents were married on a yacht.* (They weren't.) *The wedding dress is in the attic.* (It wasn't.)

Grandma was a fabulist known for regaling us with elaborate stories from her life, like the time she went to King George's coronation in England with her then-husband, Sir Rodgers. (We think there were three husbands, but we're not totally sure.) Accordingly, her explanations about my biological father's absence were similarly grand, unverifiable, and ever changing.

More than once, I listened to her yarn-spinning and thought, *Really?* Even as a child, I knew to take her stories about my mythical father with a hefty grain of salt. Perhaps she just wanted me to believe that fairy tales were possible (well, except for the one about the plane crash).

But as far as I was concerned, there was no magic to be found—only the gaping hole of paternal absence.

I never fact-checked these stories with my mother, because not talking about *him* was one of our unspoken rules. Like a lot of kids, I didn't have to be explicitly told that this topic was off-limits. I could sense her pain and trauma around whatever had happened between them. The last thing I wanted was to add more hurt, risking distance between me and the only parent I had. So I resigned myself to waiting. When I was older, I'd figure out the truth on my own. Meanwhile, his searing absence seemed to grow hotter every year. More years without a father didn't lessen the pain; in fact, my loneliness grew, especially when I compared myself to my friends' families. My family was not a "normal" family. And that meant that I wasn't "normal," either.

Then Ken arrived.

To my amazement, Ken was much better than "normal." His presence and care helped fill the paternal hole in my heart with a stable, consistent love I had never known. He came to my after-school activities and parent-teacher conferences. And yes, he took me out for sundaes, but not after I received As on my report card (which I never did). Instead, he would take me out after I had owned my screw-ups, like the time I admitted to shoplifting a barrette at the mall. My mom wanted to murder me, but Ken calmed her down and then took me and the stolen accessory to the store manager so I could apologize. He had the good sense to know my sheer embarrassment would be enough to cure my sticky fingers—which it did. In all my earlier father fantasies, I hadn't known that what I really wanted was a dad who *got* me, who not only saw me for me but loved me for me.

Four years after I made fun of his mustache, Ken adopted me, officially becoming my father.

For the big day, my mom let me buy an outfit with little embroidered golf balls on it—my way of showing him that I cared about the stuff he loved and was grateful to be included in his heart.

Mom and Dad parented very differently. She took my every teenage whim seriously. Whereas he never bit. For example, when I wanted to change my name to Jasmine, it drove her nuts: "Kristin, *I* named you Kristin for a reason! Jasmine is not a name; it is a *flower!*" This, of course, made me want to be Jasmine even more. Meanwhile, when I floated the topic at dinner, Dad would slowly nod and say, "Jasmine. That's a nice name."

On the long-awaited day when I officially became a daughter who had a father, Dad figured out how to put Jasmine behind us once and for all. We were in the judge's chamber when he turned to me with his big smile and said, "Now's your chance to officially become Jasmine Carr."

I never uttered the name Jasmine again.

Year after year, Dad exceeded all my dreams of what a father should be. To go from the pain and neglect of having no father to having one like Dad felt like nothing short of a miracle. And every time he showed up for me (the occasions too numerous to count) with a reassuring "It will be OK," I was reminded of that miracle. And yet, the mystery around my biological father continued to be a source of pain as I grew into a young adult.

BROKEN ROAD

A few years after the adoption, Dad and Mom drove me, at my request, to meet the fella responsible for 50 percent of my genetic material—my bio dad.

By this time, some details about my BD had been fleshed out and verified. Over the years, Alice, a close friend of my paternal grandmother, Phyllis, would invite me over for tea and give me little trinkets from Phyllis, a landscape painter and an heir to a railroad fortune. That last part explained why my maternal grandmother made such a fuss about these sporadic visits, dressing me in handmade outfits (with endless ruffles), ostensibly to impress Phyllis by way of Alice's recounting. Before our first meeting, my mother gently explained, in the sparest of terms, Alice's connection to BD. *Oh*, I remember thinking. That made me try doubly hard to wow her.

Once, on a visit with Alice, I forgot to put my teacup in the saucer, and it left a ring mark on her mahogany table, which *mortified* me. Even though I was young, these visits felt high stakes, like BD might actually want to get to know me after hearing Alice's glowing reports (if only I hadn't damaged her fancy furniture). But as it turns out, those visits were kept secret from BD, who had forbidden his mother to have any contact with her only granddaughter.

So *that* explained the hush-hush, don't-talk-about-that-guy vibe I'd been picking up on my whole life.

Pieces of the real story kept coming. Eventually, I learned that my biological father hit the road not long after my mother told him she was pregnant with his baby. From that point on he spoke through lawyers who made it clear to my frightened and heartbroken young mother that he wanted nothing to do with us—especially me.

At the age of 18, even though it felt risky, I decided to write Phyllis a letter. I didn't want much from her—just a photo of my father so my brain could fill in at least that one blank: *Did I look like him?* On my maternal side, the women in my family all have dark shiny hair, olive skin, and big boobs. My hair and complexion are right out of an '80s Def Leppard video. And the boobs? Let's just say they skipped a generation.

As fate would have it, Phyllis died before receiving my letter. Even though I'd never known her, Phyllis's loss unleashed so many untapped feelings. Sorrow for experiences I didn't get to have with her and resentment that BD kept me from my grandmother. Finally, I snapped.

Raging at my mom, I yelled, "If he doesn't want to know me, then he'll have to tell me why himself!" I'm sure the last thing she wanted was to come face-to-face with an ex who abandoned her during her pregnancy. Yet in my fury, she could see that there was no getting around his shadowy presence anymore. So my mother conceded and reached out to him directly. Thankfully, BD's wife was very supportive of the idea and paved the way for our connection.

As my parents and I reached the end of BD's driveway on Broken Road, I had my first of many subsequent panic attacks. I was about to meet the man whose absence had shaped and determined my life, and I had no clue how it was going to go. What if I flipped out and told him off? What if he did that to me? All my internalized rejection and grief swelled to the surface until I could barely breathe.

Sensing my distress, Dad reassured me, as he always did. "It will be OK," he said, putting his hand on mine. "And if you don't want to do this, we can just turn the car around and go home. We'll take 95 to 495 and then we sail right onto 84." As a lifelong road warrior who owned an asphalt-recycling paving business, Dad always included directions with advice, toasts, and escape plans.

"Whatever you choose," he continued, *"I'm* your dad, and I'll be right by your side, now and always."

Dad's support made it possible for me to go through with the visit, which, though awkward, went better than expected. There's a lot more to unpack here, and we'll get to it later on—not surprisingly, in chapter 5, "Grief & Trauma: The Golden Repair." Looking back, what strikes me now is not so much the memory of meeting my bio dad for the first time but more so Dad's constant, loving presence throughout this difficult and tension-filled encounter with a man I wasn't sure wanted anything to do with me. Like always, he had my back. Like always, he made whatever was "not OK" less so.

BE GENTLE WITH YOURSELF

After silencing the jackhammers, I settled into my parents' softly lit living room and thought back to eavesdropping on Dad repeating, "It will be OK. I will be OK." Unbeknownst to me then, these would be some of Dad's last words. I couldn't stop thinking about them.

Will it really *be OK?* I wondered. I wanted to believe that my dad was right, but sometimes life felt impossible.

In addition to Dad dying, I had a whole list of crap that didn't always feel OK: living with my own stage IV cancer diagnosis for close to half my life, dealing with a global pandemic, watching my business falter as Dad's health went into steep decline, and managing my depression, which was so familiar it sometimes felt like an annoying friend. The awakening of old traumas and family dramas.

And this on top of the social, political, and economic shit show of the last few years.

Did I mention perimenopause? *Fuck.* I was definitely *not* OK. These stresses were taking a toll (and draining the collagen out of my face). No wonder Dad's mantra hit me on so many levels. What would it require for me to give that kind of comfort to myself?

If I thought I could muscle my way out of my next dark night of the soul, I had another thing coming.

BEING OK STARTS WITH ACKNOWLEDGING THAT, IN FACT, YOU ARE NOT OK

So often we miss this step or avoid the truth of how we actually are. There's so much pressure to be *grrreat!*—happy, wise, and in control—that we have a hard time sitting with our internal reality. Instead, we cover up angst by racing forward, looking for people, things, and solutions outside ourselves—as if we are problems to be fixed. In truth, we are not broken. We do not need fixing. We just need loving.

Dad's path to OK-ness included a kind of self-love that I'd sporadically tried to give myself, ever since my own cancer wake-up call in 2003. He could no longer pretend to be fine. He stopped avoiding difficult conversations for fear of their repercussions. And he refused to ignore his physical and emotional needs. He didn't force himself to trudge through another evening out because so-and-so would be disappointed when what he really needed was to sink into his La-Z-Boy and watch golf.

I was lucky to have a front-row seat to his heart as he shed tears, had vulnerable conversations, and tied up worldly loose ends. I watched as he forgave himself and others, and slowly swatted away old nagging regrets, like tiny gnats buzzing around his shoulder.

He was open about finally letting go of the chronic anxiety that had plagued him throughout his life—the big stuff he'd spent years wishing he could change, as well as the "agonizing reappraisals," or what he called ARs for short, those cringey moments you wish you could take back. Like when you have one too many champagne cocktails at a party and tell the obnoxious hostess what you *really* think of her.

It took a lot of guts for him to become more himself as he neared death—faults, fragilities, tumors, and all.

The emotional shifts he made during this time gave me a beautiful example of what self-acceptance actually looks like. And that was striking, especially considering the formidable challenges brought on by his illness. Here he was riddled with cancer, unable to feed or bathe himself, sporting magic underwear (my name for his adult diapers), and yet becoming more OK and more loving toward himself with each fleeting day.

In my career as an author and speaker, I've had the privilege of sharing some of the biggest stages with the titans of transformation. But in those final years of his life, Dad's presence and wisdom went far beyond anything I'd ever experienced.

WELCOME YOUR GRIEF HOME

Losing a parent is devastating at any age. For better or worse, our parents inform who we are and how we live and love. A parent's death prompts a cascade of existential angst, right alongside the grief we experience. Despite the magnitude of this kind of loss, most of us never really talk about this experience. It's as if there's an unspoken rule that parents die first. It's the natural order of things, so we should just keep quiet about the storms that may be brewing inside. Once the memorial is over and we've finished eating the shrimp casserole the neighbor dropped off, we move on. Back to the grind and the groceries.

But what happens when the groceries remind us of that time we made root beer floats together and watched the Chicago Cubs win their first World Series championship since 1908? I'll tell you, we crack wide open and don't feel OK or normal talking about our anguish. Instead, we go radio silent.

For me, there was this sense that if I talked about my grief past an acceptable period of time (whatever *that* is), I would seem childish and immature or, worse, tedious. Those beliefs kept me silenced. I didn't want to be a burden or a bummer; no one does.

In the wake of my dad's passing, there's a part of me that will never be OK. There's a hole in my heart that will always need my care and attention. I can't fully move on and I never will. But in embracing my grief, I can begin to imagine what moving forward might look like.

While there's no time limit on grief, we also don't want it to dominate our lives to the point that there isn't room for much else. The hope is to extend grief an ongoing invitation to come home whenever it needs comfort—just like a loving parent would offer their child when they needed support.

Even when we're grown-ass humans, we all still have moments of feeling like little kids on the inside. When we ache, we want to be soothed, especially by our primary caregivers. We want to know that it will be OK, and so will we.

The loss of our parents is one of the most destabilizing and emotionally significant experiences we will ever go through. It kicks up deep feelings of fear and abandonment, wounds and behaviors that are passed down in our very DNA. It changes both our lives and our brains (which we'll explore in a coming chapter). It's OK to actually feel the immensity of this loss. It doesn't go away, just like our love doesn't go away. But over time, the waves get easier to surf. Especially when we remember the love as much as, if not more than, the grief.

CASH-ONLY BAR

Sometime after the jackhammer incident, when the veil kept getting thinner by the day, Dad caught me as I was walking out of his room.

"Kristin?" he called. His voice was soft but serious.

Assuming he needed water or more pain meds, I turned and said, "Yeah, Dad?"

"Remember," he shared in his morphine haze, "it's a cash-only bar."

Good to know, Dad.

Now, I don't know where we go when we die or how we get there, but apparently they don't take credit cards. Pretty sure my dad wanted me to know this in case I needed to swing by an ATM. As always, he wanted to make sure I was OK.

I'm getting there.

CHAPTER 2

The Rupture

Now, every time I witness a strong person,
I want to know: What dark did you conquer in your
story? Mountains do not rise without earthquakes.

— KATHERINE MACKENETT

Have you ever had a moment of seeing your worst fears realized? Most of us have, at some point. A needle off the record of your life. Your world crumbling into a million disconnected puzzle pieces. A situation that is such a clusterf*ck that at first glance you're positive it can't be fixed. And if by some miracle you *can* make it better, you will surely never be the same.

This is what I call "the rupture."

Ruptures come in all shapes and sizes. Getting unceremoniously fired from a job. Losing a close friendship for no discernible reason. Financial instability that leads to downsizing, a breakup or divorce, or other dramatic life alterations. A loved one's health diagnosis, your own diagnosis, and so on. We can't help but fear these moments and the subsequent changes that accompany them.

But I'm here to tell you that even the worst ruptures can reveal a road map to our next chapter. While causing us dread, the unexpected ruptures in our lives can also bring our desires, values, and priorities into sharp relief, forcing us to reexamine where we've been and take urgent action that will hopefully get us where we're meant to be.

HAPPY VALENTINE'S DAY, YOU HAVE CANCER

The biggest rupture I've ever experienced was on February 14, 2003. I was 31 years old, and I had been diagnosed with a rare, stage IV cancer with no cure and no treatment.

The first doctor I met with suggested a triple-organ transplant. The next kept me waiting for three hours, rushed me through my appointment, and suggested radical treatments that wouldn't do much, he admitted. As I sat there dumbfounded, he capped off our meeting by giving me an expiration date. "You probably have around 10 years to live if you're lucky. . . . Next patient!"

Afterward, I remember standing at the elevator outside his office, pressing the down button and feeling like my life was going up in a fiery blaze before my very eyes. But as anxiety prone as I can be, my loop of panicked thoughts went quiet. In their place, I could hear a calming and grounding inner voice coming straight from my heart. *No. You need more information. Better information.*

That voice lifted me up when I needed it most, and right then and there, I decided to become the CEO of my health, to build a game plan and team to support me. I called my new company "Save My Ass Technologies, Inc.," and went about interviewing, hiring, and firing until I found the ideal candidate to be my second-in-command— an oncologist who saw me as a whole person and would go on to support me, body, mind, and spirit. They had to know the most about my rare shit pickle of an illness, have their finger on the pulse of research, and, of course, be kind. (No douchebags allowed.)

After a long hunt, I finally found my wingman, Dr. D. With a positive and steady demeanor, he explained that sometimes my disease was slow growing and other times quite aggressive. How it would affect me would be a mystery, so he suggested a "watch and wait—let cancer make the first move" approach. We'd monitor my progress and hope for the slow-growing variety. If it became aggressive at some point, there might be treatment options available down the line. Fingers crossed.

"And while we're watching and waiting," Dr. D. said, "you watch and *live*. Take care of yourself."

Was the good doctor high on his own stash? I had no idea how the hell to do that. To me, "healthy living" up until this point was forgoing the large fries for a medium at Burger King or bumming cigarettes instead of buying my own pack—habits that felt very necessary and comforting at the time.

Even if I was lucky enough to have the slow-growing variety, living with never-ending cancer was like having anxiety on steroids. As I pondered Dr. D.'s parting words, I thought, *How am I going to live with cancer without panicking about dying every day?*

At the time, I was still picking up the pieces of a broken engagement to the person I thought I was going to spend the rest of my life with and was just figuring out how to be on my own again. I had no desire to embark on some

Joseph Campbell–themed hero's journey, which would require exploring some of life's big questions, on top of my already aching heart.

But thanks to the rupture, that's not what happened.

OUT OF THE FRYING PAN, INTO THE FIRE

After the meeting with Dr. D., I went directly to Whole Foods Market (which I quickly took to calling "Whole Paycheck Market") and never looked back. I knew there would be so much coming my way that would be out of my control, but what I could impact was what I ate and how I cared for myself. So I took my fear and channeled it into a healing game plan. Action was progress. Action kept me operational. Action made me eat fiber.

I immediately became a voracious student of integrative health. The more I learned about the regenerative power of an anti-inflammatory diet and lifestyle, the more I shared my findings with anyone who would listen. My mind was *blown*. I was awestruck by how our bodies work and their enormous capacity for resilience. (We'll nerd out on this more in Chapter 11.)

To my amazement, my passion for wellness eventually led me to make an award-winning film about my journey, which featured stories of other young women who were also living with cancer. After the film I wound up writing a series of *New York Times* best-selling books and launching a global online wellness community that has provided education and support to thousands of people around the world. I was also featured on *Oprah* several times and became a member of her Super Soul 100, "a group of 100 trailblazers whose vision and life's work are bringing a higher level of consciousness to the world."

In so many ways, the rupture of my diagnosis led me to build a more meaningful life. (And bonus: this is where I first connected with my husband, Brian, who was the editor of my film. So in the end, the love story that was meant for me was born of my darkest moment.)

Now, close to two decades later, I still *live* with stage IV cancer. Knock on wood, it continues to be slow growing, which has allowed me to continue figuring out how to best take care of myself and help others do the same.

Change is a constant, though. Just because we have one rupture in life doesn't mean that life will never get turned upside down again. A few years before my dad's diagnosis, I started to realize that as amazing as my accomplishments were, and as strong as my physical health had become, deep down I was mentally and emotionally exhausted. I'd gone from the frying pan of a cancer diagnosis to the fire of nonstop achievement.

For me, prolonged "busy" looked like very long hours at work, while attempting to also manage my health and try to squeeze in time with my family and close friends. This go-go pace had become like breathing to me, autonomic—reflexive, involuntary—which isn't such a surprise. In times of rupture, staying busy can be useful—even therapeutic—because it helps us keep up or return to some sense of "normal life."

Sounds about right to me—unless "busy" becomes a knee-jerk way to avoid our own feelings or allows us to find agoraphobia just this side of glamorous. No matter how necessary, noble, or lifesaving it may seem, when busyness becomes a permanent state of being, it undoubtedly leads to burnout, health issues, and even worse—loss of joy.

As a wellness expert, I certainly knew better than to accept and live within this perpetual grind. Yet, a deeper part of me worried that if I paused to really hear what my inner self was saying ("Slow down!"), my world as I knew it would fall apart. The cancer would catch up. My business would fail. I'd disappoint the people in my life and forget to wear pants in public—the list went on and on.

And yet, the 31-year-old me who started this journey was now the 50-year-old me, who existed in a very different place, with very different needs. I knew something had to give when I occasionally found myself fantasizing about getting sicker, as if another wake-up call would give me an undeniable excuse to stop and press reset—again. Whoa. While never a comfortable place to find ourselves, hoping that catastrophic scenarios come to pass is an undeniable data point.

Maybe you, too, have found yourself casually day-dreaming about rupture, thinking that this is what it would take to effect any kind of real change. You wish that the medical report (or XYZ) would be bad (just not *too* bad) so you can finally carve out time to take care of yourself. You secretly pray you'll find evidence of your spouse's infidelity so you don't have to own up to the fact that the partnership no longer serves you. There are so many worst-case scenarios that could, in some ways, make our lives "easier" by giving us the kick in the butt we won't give ourselves. I get it. But we can't outsource our happiness, hoping that life will do the heavy lifting for us.

Looking back, I can now see that I didn't fully understand just how much unprocessed and repressed grief and trauma I was carrying. It was as if a part of me was frozen and I had no idea how to help her, even though I thought I did. But years later, my system was still in shock—still recovering from suddenly being thrust into a world I didn't know, with an identity I didn't want, and a future that terrified me. I just hadn't stopped long enough or developed the awareness to recognize how traumatic this all was. I was too busy trying to stay alive.

Facing Dad's sickness ripped those old wounds wide open, unleashing stored pain hiding in my body and behaviors, as well as new fears about losing him—something I'd never even contemplated.

READY, SET, RUPTURE

Dad's cancer arrived without warning.

I pulled into my parents' driveway around midnight, taking them up on their offer to crash at their place after my nearby flight had been delayed. As I got out of the car, I noticed that all the lights in the house were on—my first clue something was wrong.

Uh-oh. I felt a pang in my stomach.

Mom greeted me at the door, fully dressed in "slacks" and a matching sweater set—second clue. Slacks meant business, especially when worn late at night.

As she hugged me and asked about my trip, I answered her briefly ("Fine") while surveying her face for clues. Her eyes looked strained. Something was definitely up.

"Listen, there's something I need to tell you," she said as I was taking off my shoes. Then she paused for 10 unbearable seconds.

"I don't know how to say it, so I'll just say it. Dad has a mass on his pancreas, and he needs to get a biopsy first thing tomorrow."

His pancreas? Shit. Shit. Shit.

"Can I come to his biopsy with you? And can I stay for as long as it takes to figure this shit out?" I asked.

"Oh, yes. Please," she responded. We hugged and cried and then we did what the women in my family do—we put on our fucking game faces and (you guessed it!) got busy.

Spreadsheets. Research. Facebook groups. Phone calls. E-mails. Second and third opinions. Networking. Networking. Networking. My mom goes into beast mode with this stuff. Doctors are blown away by her thoroughness. They say things like, "I wish you could teach all my patients how to organize like this." But like all beasts, Mom has teeth and she will use them.

For example, don't tell her she can't have a physical copy of the latest round of blood work because "it isn't standard procedure." Moving mountains to save your loved ones isn't standard procedure, either. Get her the damn report. Unfortunately, Mom's tenacity is warranted. In today's medical system, you have to be hypervigilant to get the care you need. For people with anxiety and control issues, this is the marathon that we've been training for our whole lives. No doubt, having a trauma history plays a role, too. We're so accustomed to the chaos of crises that it feels natural and good to navigate storms. Survivors gonna survive.

My mother's fierceness and compassion are among the reasons my dad lived for as long, and as well, as he did. And this wasn't the first time she had to go into beast mode. As I watched her eagle-eyeing nurses, meticulously taking notes and formulating important follow-up questions, I was reminded of how quickly she had also flown into action in the early days of my own diagnosis. How many years of her precious life would be eaten up by caring for loved ones with cancer? I was enraged *for* her. And yet I've sometimes felt like the reason I got sick was so we'd have half a clue about what to do when Dad needed us. Turns out my cancer was our family's dress rehearsal.

I didn't sleep a wink that night, and I don't remember what I said to Dad the next morning. What I *do* remember was his biopsy. I marveled at how dressed up he looked in his wingtips and crisp button-down shirt. In his words, "You have to look spiffy for these things."

He was still groggy as we were leaving the hospital. Seeing him looking so vulnerable was foreign territory. It reduced me to feeling like a little girl trying to imagine what a grown-up would do in this situation. *How should I act? What should I say?*

"I'm sorry your rock is a little wobbly right now," Dad whispered as I held his arm to steady his balance. I dug my nails into my palms to shove my tears back into their ducts.

"You have absolutely nothing to be sorry about, Dad. I'm lucky to be *your* rock for a change."

We sat quietly on a bench, our faces warmed by the sun, as we waited for my mom to bring the car around. After a bit, Dad turned to me with tears in his eyes. "I don't like being in this cancer club, but if there's anyone I'd want to be in it with, it's you."

"Ditto, Dad," I said. "I hate that you're in the club with me, but we'll do this together."

That I was sure of.

THE QUESTION ISN'T WHY—IT'S WHAT

Dad getting cancer didn't make any sense. It was the summer of 2016, and he had been feeling great, working out with a trainer, and in very good shape for a 67-year-old man. His body was lean, his diet was healthy, and he was actively managing his stress better by learning to meditate (thanks to my mom). I couldn't help but ask, *Why Dad?*

The difficult thing I've learned about getting caught up in the "why" of any curveball is that this question is rarely answered. But I get it. It's hard for us humans to accept that there are many things we don't know, can't know, or may never know. Instead, we like to fill in the mystery with our own clever, overactive imaginations. In fact, it's one of the things our brains are designed to do—look at the past and scan it for clues in order to create risk assessments. The more we're able to troubleshoot, the better chance we have at survival. The problem is, when our brains don't have enough data, they can get anxious and make shit up. Cue the cuckoo—or is that just me?

In the early days of my own diagnosis, I wondered what I had done to cause my cancer. Was I too angry or moody? Did I eat too many processed foods or enjoy a little too much cocaine in the '90s? Perhaps it was karma for sending an adult sex toys catalog to my uptight school principal?

If I could only figure out *why* cancer was in my body, maybe I could stop it—a reasonable desire but one that wasn't serving my mental health long-term. Head-tripping 24-7 over an unanswerable question was definitely not productive.

In the decades since my diagnosis, I've learned that "What?" is a better question to ask than "Why?" For example:

- What *is going on in my body when I have these anxious thoughts?*

- What *part of my body feels the most scared or anxious?*

- What *can I do to support myself now?*

- What *helps me de-escalate my worry in healthy ways?*

Truth is, we may never know why we or someone we love gets sick. Why our partner decides to leave us for a younger lover. Why we get laid off from a dream job or booted from a once-in-a-lifetime opportunity. Why a BFF suddenly becomes distant. Why a seemingly good financial investment goes south. And on and on. And while assigning blame may make us feel like we have some degree of control, ultimately it's the *last* thing that deserves to be taking up valuable space in our minds. Survival demands that we don't get stuck looking back or spinning our wheels with worry about the future or beating ourselves to a pulp with a bunch of "should-haves."

When it comes to navigating uncertain moments, a far more productive focus is on how we care for our mental and physical health, right here and right now. When we let go of the "why" and zero in on the "what"—as in, *What do I most need right now to feel supported?*—we not only calm our systems, but we become more present, more adaptable, more creative, and, most importantly, more at ease with life's natural currents.

HOLD FAST

Only 1 in 10 pancreatic cancer patients survives five years past their diagnosis. If the cancer is found early and the tumor can be removed, the chances for survival are slightly higher. But one of the problems with pancreatic cancer is that it's hard to detect because the symptoms often go overlooked.

Dad's disease was already aggressive when the doctors found it. If he didn't do chemo and radiation right away, his prognosis of survival was less than two months. To make matters worse, his tumor was wrapped around a major artery. The only way he'd even be eligible for surgery was if the mass shrank enough to clear the artery.

Dad muscled through six months of a powerful cocktail of chemotherapy and radiation, along with all their debilitating side effects. To help him find the inner strength to dig deep, my mother made a beautiful altar with photos of our ancestors, cherished mementos that reminded him that life was so worth fighting for. She also framed a photo of his personal mantra: *Hold fast*—a nautical term that to him meant "rough seas ahead, tie the lines, batten down the hatches."

Each morning my parents would sit at their sacred altar and meditate on those words. They'd read inspirational books, practice gratitude, and connect with each other outside the blur of medical terminology and doctors' appointments. During this time, I watched as the irritations and preoccupations they had with life and each other slowly faded into the background and were replaced by a deep and abiding sense of what truly mattered: love.

Every other week, I watched Dad hold fast and gin up the motivation to get hooked up to chemo. He'd visualize his tumor as a snowball—blessing the medicine as it entered his body and melted the tumor. For someone who often struggled with anxiety, you'd think this terrifying experience would have only exacerbated his nerves. And yet, the process of allowing himself to be more open, honest, and vulnerable (aka allowing himself to be himself) helped him heal in ways that went far beyond his physical body.

By May of 2017, Dad's courage and fortitude paid off. The tumor had shrunk enough for him to be eligible to receive the Whipple procedure—a complicated seven-hour surgery that would extend his life.

At 5 A.M. sharp, we met him in the lobby of the hotel across the street from the hospital. Though it was only a two-minute walk, he wanted to arrive early (and spiffy), like always and for everything. Dad was nervous but hopeful. He even skipped along the sidewalk—his way of showing us that even though big shit was about to go down, he was still Dad. Still the guy who always tried to make the best of every situation. Cancer might take a bunch of his organs (part of his pancreas, small intestine, spleen, his gallbladder, and bile duct), but it couldn't take his spirit. Dad being Dad buoyed our spirits, too.

"They just started, and all is well," the nurse assigned to us reported, as we huddled in the family lounge, waiting for news from the operating room.

"He's halfway through, and so far, so good . . ."

"It's going to take a little longer because the tumor was closer to the vein than expected, but they're still on track. About an hour to go, and then the doctor will speak to you."

Between these nail-biter briefings, we tried to distract ourselves by creating an ultimate movie guide list on my phone. For me, action and thrillers. For Mom, movies about dogs. For Brian, Turner Classics and anything with subtitles (or what I call "cinema Ambien").

Somewhere between *Citizen Kane* and *Marley & Me*, Dad's surgeon emerged. "I got it all," he said. "We'll need to do some more chemo as an insurance policy, but as of now, he's in remission."

Ohthankgod. I exhaled so fully I thought I'd deflate. I'm not sure I've ever felt so fortunate as I did at that moment. Mom was a puddle of relief. Brian acted like an ecstatic sports announcer whose favorite team had just scored—*gooooal!*

Dad didn't want anyone but my mother to tell him the news. In case it was bad, she was the only person he felt comfortable sharing the moment with. He greeted me with a huge, anesthesia-laced grin when I was finally allowed to see him. We laughed. We cried. Above all, we were grateful. Dad thanked his amazing surgeon for saving his life. And then he told us about a dream he had. "It was the craziest experience. I was in an epic sword fight," he said.

"Guess what, Dad?" I replied. "You won."

PEOPLE AREN'T PROJECTS

Post surgery, you'd think my anxiety would have eased up a bit, especially after the fantastic news. But it actually got worse. Rather than find comfort (or at least a respite) in the successful outcome, I let perpetual worry about Dad relapsing worm its way into my brain. So, naturally, I numbed that feeling by planning, strategizing, and trying to take control.

Don't get me wrong—strategizing and planning are extremely helpful, especially in life-threatening situations. I wouldn't be here writing this book if I didn't have these skills. In many ways, I can thank my anxiety for helping save my life. But when my anxiety becomes acute and pervasive, it not only affects my physical well-being; it clouds my ability to make sound decisions. According to research, our brains think and plan more effectively when we're *not* anxious, which makes perfect sense. Have you ever tried to make an important decision or solve a challenging problem while freaking out? The outcome can be "interesting," to say the least.

To make matters worse, I wasn't aware of how my behavior was putting undue stress and pressure on others—especially my parents.

My focus remained on "fixing" Dad. I was too busy calling in all my troops. Top integrative doctors weighed in. Out-of-the-box adjunct treatments were recommended. Dietitians built specific meal plans designed to rebuild Dad's body. Books were purchased, supplements were ordered, acupuncture appointments were scheduled. Medical marijuana was approved (or as Dad called it, "grass," a term no one has used since 1969).

Mom and I went into overdrive to secure everything. There was just one problem: Dad wasn't up for any of it. The debilitating treatments and side effects he was already experiencing were all he could handle. But he didn't want to seem ungrateful or to let anyone down, so he'd act like he was interested in what we had to offer him. Then, when it came time to actually go to the acupuncturist or eat the carefully curated diet, he'd decline, saying, "Not right now."

At first, his rain checks didn't faze me. But as they began to pile up, I realized that "not right now" was Dad's way of saying he'd had enough. In reality, Mom was over capacity with his round-the-clock needs, too. Plus, she was experiencing her own fear, anxiety, and caregiver fatigue. But instead of pausing and honoring where they were at, my anxiety drove me to keep searching, trying, pushing.

I'll never forget the look on their faces when we met the nutritionist assigned to us at the local hospital where Dad got his follow-up treatments. "Wait, are you *Kris Carr*? Who wrote all those books about cancer? Wow, OK, just do whatever *she* says, you're in great hands!" This was the last thing either of my parents wanted to hear.

It reminded me of my first Thanksgiving after going vegan as part of my cancer-fighting regimen. I couldn't stop yammering about the benefits of a plant-based diet. As always, my parents were troupers. They even made a bunch of vegan dishes to share. All was well until an actual cooked turkey came out. Suddenly, the newbie vegan activist in me decided it was the perfect time to preach a sermon on the intersection of health, ethics, and the environment. Why my lecture fell flat was a mystery to me.

"Love," Dad said, "I know you're passionate about this stuff, and we're on board and even willing to try it ourselves—I mean, not all the way, but a lot. But if you want your message to resonate with people, you can't pound them over the head. Ease up. You have to meet them where they are."

Translation: don't be a dick and ruin Thanksgiving.

He was right. Nobody wants to be told how to live—and they definitely don't want to be forced to change. In fact, the only time you can change someone is when they're in diapers. Yet there I was, wagging my finger about how superior my compassionate choices were, while failing to extend that same compassion to my family.

And now here I was, years later, trying to fix Dad's food and control his lifestyle in an effort to calm my anxiety and make cancer leave him alone. I wasn't interested in what he wanted or what his body could tolerate, because my fear of losing him was superseding my ability to put his needs first. While his rupture caused another rupture in my life, it didn't give me carte blanche to override his preferences.

Cleary, my worries needed a similar heart-to-heart. *Don't be a dick and ruin the time you have left with your dad.*

To meet him where he was, I'd have to accept *his* needs while learning how to manage my own fear and anxiety.

CARING FOR YOURSELF IN TIMES OF RUPTURE

There's no "good" or "bad" or "right" or "wrong" way to handle ruptures. What matters is that you pay attention to the pleas of your heart. Here are a few more ideas to help ground and nourish you as you navigate this storm.

Create a sacred physical space: Taking inspiration from my mom's altar, I invite you to create a sacred space or area to help you connect with yourself. My mom makes the most beautiful altars with photos of family members, orchids and amaryllis plants, precious mementos, and prayer cards. Her altar holds spiritual text, runes, and soulful sayings that remind her that the universe is always loving, supporting, and guiding us, especially on our darkest days.

Let your altar or sacred space be a respite for you. A place that allows you to hear and heed the voice of your inner wisdom. Anoint it with symbols of what matters most in your life. Take time out of your day to visit this space, allowing it to replenish you.

Ask "What" instead of "Why": I know I discussed this earlier in the chapter, but it bears repeating. Life is full of uncertainties, and we may never know the reasons for some of the challenging situations we face. Rather than assigning blame and dwelling on the past, remember that it's more productive to focus on taking care of our mental and physical health in the present moment.

Instead of asking "why," we should focus on "what" we can do now. And what we need in order to feel supported.

By doing so, we become more adaptable, creative, and at ease with the natural ups and downs of life.

Get support *before* you think you need it: I'll repeat this suggestion later in the book, because it's so important. I know you're probably amazing at putting on your cape and caring for the world, but . . . you may underestimate the toll this experience will take on you, your health, and your mental well-being. It's OK to ask for help and start lining up support. To tell people what's happening and let them know that you may need a hand along the way. I wish I did this sooner, but when the next rupture comes along (and it will), I'll make sure to reread my own advice.

CHAPTER 3

Fear & Anxiety

I've had a lot of worries in my life,
most of which never happened.

— MARK TWAIN

I'm afraid of more things than I should be. I'm afraid of walking on ice, riding my bike downhill, eating sweet and savory foods in the same bite—pizza with pineapple . . . terrifying. I'm afraid the UPS guy will catch me without a bra on when he delivers my Amazon packages. I'm afraid of astronomy—the vastness of the universe, and all the math it takes to figure it out leaves me anxious and confused, wanting to kick inanimate objects. I'm afraid of having to unexpectedly talk to my neighbors. Please don't just stop by to say hello. I will need a cold compress to recover.

And at the same time, when the shit hits the fan, I'm clearly the kinda girl you want on your cleanup crew. I've had some version of an emergency "go bag" packed and ready since I was five years old. Detailed contingency plans are my love language. Trying to imagine and plan for the unimaginable helps me feel safe—or, at the very least, productive.

Think about it. Even if you can't do a darn thing about the chaos du jour that triggers your anxiety, you can still worry about it—which at least feels like you're doing *something*.

I used to think that anxiety just came naturally to me. You know how some people are born with amazing voices or athletic prowess? Well, I was born to worry. Early childhood trauma around neglect and abandonment allowed my abilities to flourish. And because I was raised by anxious people, my talents were further developed. On any given day, I could provide a litany of reasons why I was always moments away from being abducted. So, when I got sick, my fear and anxiety spread like a venereal disease.

IMAGINATION OVERLOAD

Back in 2003, before my oncologist had established a baseline for how aggressive my disease was, I got scanned every two months. Like many cancer patients, I found it hard not to think of cancer 24-7, especially when I was plagued with scanxiety—creepy, weepy worries about the results.

Like a superstitious athlete, on days when I had scans I would perform rituals to try to bend the universe toward my success (survival). I'd roll into the hospital sporting my lucky underwear—for whatever reason, my test results were better when I wore the red pair with yellow stars. Tom Brady wore the same shoulder pads since college. Wayne Gretzky always put on the right side of his hockey gear first. Michael Jordan wore his UNC shorts under his NBA shorts for every game. And Serena Williams never changed her socks during a tournament. If game-day voo-doo worked for these megahumans, then maybe my draw-ers could help me.

Cancer can do weird shit to your noggin—just like grief. Not only were my routines vital to my sanity, I also had to learn how to coexist with both rational and irratio-nal fear. Every weird ache, gas pain, or sneeze could send me into a hysterical tailspin.

Anne Lamott basically summed up my experience when she wrote, "My mind is a bad neighborhood that I try not to go into alone."

One minute I was centered, calm, and present. Feeling my butt on the chair. Paying attention to my breathing. Noticing my peaceful surroundings—a cardinal at my birdfeeder. The next minute I'd be planning the guest list for my funeral.

What kind of food would be served? Should there be a DJ? No. Not classy enough. Who should get my good jew-elry? My mom and goddaughter. Will Brian remember to feed our dogs? Brian is so lonely now. I love Brian. Maybe he should start dating again? But *not* someone younger and prettier than me. *Oh my God*, Brian is dating a hot 20-year-old! I hate Brian.

If I had enough awareness to recognize what my brain was actually doing and why, I'd meet my fear and anxiety with compassion (and a hearty chuckle). But more often than not, my negative fantasies would hold my brain hos-tage, and the next time Brian asked me if I knew where his glasses were, I'd tell him to consult his child bride.

We humans are extremely creative creatures. Our imag-inations have allowed us to invent microscopes to peer into the smallest cells of our bodies and rocket ships that hurtle us into the realm of the stars. But our imaginations can also freak us the fuck out.

Think about it, is there anything scarier than all the awful stories we tell ourselves? We're so damn good at devising the most frightening tales. Yet most of us have no desire to be Stephen King, channeling our darkest thoughts into best-selling horror novels. Instead, we do our best to bury our paranoid thoughts in the boneyard of our psyche and desperately try to become "fearless," an impossible task that goes against our very DNA.

THE RUBBER MEETS THE ROAD

As the years ticked by and my disease remained stable (not advancing enough to warrant experimental treatment that might extend my life but not fully cure me), my time between scans increased and my fear decreased.

At first my tests moved to every three months, then six months, then finally a year—which felt like a lifetime. With each graduation, I was better able to settle into my new life as a long-haul patient. When my scans got pushed to every two years, it was as if I'd won the lottery and might actually be able to go the distance with my incurable disease.

But in the days before Dad was admitted to Massachusetts General Hospital for his Whipple surgery, my fear and anxiety roared back with a vengeance. I was down the street at the Dana-Farber Cancer Institute getting my two-year checkup while Dad was getting ready to go back under the knife. Though I'd had plenty of experience with scans, too many to even count, my nerves were extra raw. Maybe it was because I was nervous for Dad. Maybe I was rattled by the small lump I'd recently found on my arm. *Had my disease finally woken up and spread further?* Whatever the reason, moments like these are when the rubber meets the road. All the mindset tools I'd cultivated stood ready for deployment.

My heart was practically beating out of my chest as Brian and I checked in to get my scan results—my cue to find a private bathroom and glue myself together before things got worse. First, I focused on my breath. Next, I took a mental inventory of all the things that were *right* with my body. Sure, I had dozens of tumors in my lungs and liver, a strange lump on my arm, and a very vivid imagination, but there were sooo many parts of me that were working exceptionally well—including the parts that were struggling. In fact, there were way more things right with me than wrong.

Finally, I reached for the strongest medicine in my toolkit: self-love. I looked in the bathroom mirror, and with all the compassion I could muster, I said: "I love you, Kris. I am here for you. Whatever happens, we'll figure it out together."

When I first started telling myself stuff like this, I felt like a big cheeseball. *Thank God no one can see me.* But I could soon see how words of self-love really worked. So I repeated them over and over until I was relaxed enough to get my ass back to the waiting area in time to be escorted to the room I knew by heart. Three chairs, a privacy curtain, and an exam table with a disposable paper sheet (presumably in case you shit yourself). I took my usual seat, fixed my eyes on the doorknob, and silently repeated my bathroom mantras.

As soon as Dr. D., my good-natured oncologist, entered, I felt a spike of adrenaline. This was the moment. Good news or bad, my body was jacked. One of the things I appreciate about Dr. D. is his bedside manner. He always bounces into the room with a smile on his face and gets right to it. No excruciating small talk.

"Hey! Good to see you. So, everything looks really great," he said.

Every cell of my body relaxed as he continued on: "We're thrilled with how well you're *still* doing. If you feel comfortable enough, we're confident that it would be safe for you to have even more time between scans. You can come back in three to five years if you want—whatever works for you."

Sweet Jesus.

After comparing 16 years of my scans, the doctors' consensus was that my cancer was stable enough to give me more breathing room between checkups.

"Are you serious!?" I exclaimed. "This is incredible! Thank you so much, Dr. D.! I'll be back in five."

The force of my enthusiastic response surprised even me. But after nearly two decades of anxiety-provoking doctors' appointments, I was ready to leave fear in my rearview.

As I was doing a happy dance in my head, Brian interjected: "Let's go with three." For him, five years felt like too much time to allow, as cancer can be a trickster and show up at the most unlikely times.

Oh, and the lump in my arm? Turns out it was a glamorous fatty tumor. No metastasis.

That night Brian and I toasted my milestone with an expensive glass of champagne at a fancy hotel bar. Perhaps I could even retire my lucky underwear (the elastic had certainly seen better days).

When I called my parents to share the news, they were ecstatic. These were the kinds of calls they prayed for.

Despite the outward celebration, on the inside I felt awful—guilty. It seemed cruel that I was OK while Dad's fate hung in the balance. My incredible news felt as if I were intentionally pouring alcohol on his open wound. *This isn't fair! Why me? Why not him? Why ask why? I know better.*

While my fear of dying was fading to a more manageable level, my fear of losing Dad was on the rise. I knew he wasn't a statistic; he was a real person with real hopes and real potential. Just because the five-year survival rate for people with pancreatic cancer is only 10 percent didn't mean he couldn't be one of the "lucky ones." Every patient's circumstances, genetic makeup, and capacity to heal are different. But I still couldn't shake the idea that I knew where this was ultimately going. That my dad wouldn't make it.

The reality is that fear and anxiety are a huge part of loss. They're so deeply intertwined that they often get all tangled up in each other. Yet, few of us expect to feel these feelings to the degree that we do while in the thick of a crisis. But for all the panic and paralysis fear and anxiety cause, they are normal states of mind. This doesn't mean we *enjoy* feeling this way. Truly, I'd rather gnaw my arm off than get caught in one of those hideous thought cyclones. Yet lightly feather-dusting such big emotions in therapy sessions was barely scratching the surface. I'd feel better for a hot second, only to be swept away an hour later by out-of-control feelings. It was exhausting.

Because I was still a newbie at understanding the interconnected complexities of complicated emotions, I wasn't always aware of what was happening in my body or how to cope when I felt flooded. If you struggle with these strong emotions, this chapter will give you a few new perspectives and tools to soothe your system.

Let's start with the basics.

THE DIFFERENCE BETWEEN FEAR AND ANXIETY

People often confuse fear and anxiety because they can feel the same way in our bodies—the heart pounding, the sweaty palms, the racing thoughts. And while they're both designed to keep us safe, they're actually different.

Fear is automatic. It's designed to protect us from tangible and immediate threats. Fear signals a clear and present danger, prompting us to take instant action—pronto. See tiger. Run. Survive. *Voilà!* Fear has done its job. It comes on in a burst and has a beginning, middle, and end.

Though we can be afraid of something from the past or future—like getting into a car accident again or losing another job—more often than not, we confuse that kind of fear with anxiety. In fact, many of us who identify as being fearful are probably more anxious than we fully understand. That was certainly the case for me when I started teasing out these complicated emotions.

Anxiety is a nervousness, unease, or worry over things that may or may *not* happen in the future. It's the *anticipation* of a threat rather than the threat itself. It's that feeling of dread that comes over us when we think about a potential hazard, especially when we turn it over and over again in our minds.

If I speak up to my brother, like I know I must, he's going to decimate me.

If I don't get that flight out before the hurricane hits, I'm going to get stuck in Weather Channel hell.

If I quit my fancy but unsatisfying job, I'll never find anything else and wind up broke and hungry.

And while anxiety can be less intense than fear, it tends to last much longer. That's because anxiety gets triggered by uncertainty—the very nature of life.

If fear's job is to identify a threat and quickly take action, anxiety's job is to run worst-case scenarios and gauge what *could* happen, in order to come up with a plan and protect ourselves. Anxiety keeps us vigilant so we can pay attention, strategize, and stay on top of things.

Remember, all of our emotions serve a purpose. We can thank fear for helping us swerve out of the way of an oncoming car or jump when we see a snake slithering toward us. Fear makes us call 911 when our house is on fire.

We can applaud anxiety for forcing us to finally get that persistent pain checked out. Anxiety alerts us to choose another street to walk down late at night. It tells us to yell "not friendly" to the oblivious dog owner whose bouncy, untethered pooch charges toward our leashed (and salivating) pit bull. There's a reason her nickname is "Rumbles."

Anxiety can be beneficial beyond saving us from doom-and-gloom scenarios, too. In healthy doses, it can make us more productive, foster good-natured competition, and inspire us to do our best. Most importantly, anxiety reminds us to wear pants, especially in public. No anxiety, no pants.

But anxiety can also be sneaky. It manifests in many unhealthy ways, too. For example, here are two common forms that many of us can recognize: (1) we hustle harder to get shit done and feel like we're in control; or (2) we get frozen and overwhelmed so we do nothing (avoid, procrastinate, assume new identities, and move to Mexico). Both of these behaviors often lead to the same stellar result: more anxiety. It's a vicious cycle.

Both fear and anxiety naturally spring into high alert when our worlds plunge into free fall. This is to be expected—unless you're a sociopathic serial killer. They don't feel these important emotions, which is why they have no problem using a wood chipper.

In the last few years, anxiety alone has collectively sky-rocketed. Today, more than 40 million people suffer from full-blown anxiety disorders in the United States alone. Pre-pandemic the United Nations estimated that nearly 1 billion people worldwide were struggling with a mental health condition. Since then, the pandemic has caused a 25 to 27 percent increase in anxiety and depression. According to a recent Gallup poll, worry, stress, fear, anger, and sadness have been on the rise globally for the past decade and reached record highs in 2021. Something's got to give, or our bodies will.

Living in this state of heightened alert, stress, and general emotional upheaval, we feel as if our alarms won't turn off. This damages our bodies by perpetuating a prolonged stress response that weakens our immune systems, messes with our hormones, blows out our adrenals, and impacts our resilience. None of us want that, and yet, here we are.

YOUR BRAIN ON FEAR AND ANXIETY

Remember those antidrug commercials from the '80s? Maybe I'm dating myself here, but those PSAs made me scared (and hungry) at the same time.

"This is your brain," an ominous voice announces as an egg dropped into a buttery, sizzling frying pan.

"This is your brain on drugs," the voice reveals as we watch as the egg bubbles, fries, and shrinks. The crispy brown edges, an emblem of destruction.

"Any questions?" the voice demands.

Yeah. Can I get a roll and coffee with that?

I know that commercial was supposed to keep me from doing ecstasy in English class with the girl who came from an exotic place called Chicago, but it didn't.

All kidding aside, some researchers believe that chronic anxiety can not only harm your brain—it can become addictive, like a drug.

Like many women I know, my mind is built to solve problems and seek solutions. But two things can be true at once. A strength can also be a weakness when taken to the extreme.

One of my favorite experts on anxiety is Dr. Judson Brewer. Dr. Jud, as he likes to be called, is an Associate Professor in Psychiatry and the Director of Research and Innovation at the Mindfulness Center at Brown University. His studies suggest that anxiety is more habitual than we realize.

To understand his research, we first have to remember how our habits work. All habits (positive and negative) have three distinct parts: *trigger, behavior,* and *reward.* The trigger kicks off the behavior, and the behavior creates a reward or result. (FYI, I use the terms "reward" and "result" interchangeably because not all rewards are so rewarding.) For example, let's say you're feeling stressed at work (trigger). You want this feeling to go away, so you drink a few glasses of wine each night to relax (behavior). The distraction helps you temporarily feel better (reward).

According to Dr. Jud, over time negative behaviors create addictive habits that gloss over the cause of our suffering and create more problems in our lives. Enter the usual suspects: overeating, drinking, drugs, endless social media scrolling, procrastination, stress-shopping, sex with randos, and anything else you can think of to make the discomfort *stop.*

In these patterns, it's easy to see how anxiety can be similar to an addictive habit. The more we fuel it, the more anxious we get, and the more we turn to unhealthy behaviors to reduce our anxiety. It's a never-ending cycle that wears us down, shrinks our resilience, and makes our lives way smaller than they need to be.

Now for the good news: habits aren't fixed; they're fluid—just like our brains. In fact, our beautiful brains have the ability to change and form new patterns and connections throughout our lives—no matter how old we are. (That means you *can* teach old dogs new tricks. Lucky us!)

If we can understand how our brains work and what they do when we're stressed-out, scared, and worried, we can help them calm down, come back online, and create new neural pathways that lead to better resilience.

BRAIN BASICS 101

Our busy brains fire off tens of thousands of thoughts each day. As such, many of us believe that we're thinking creatures who happen to feel. Best-selling author and neuroscientist Jill Bolte Taylor argues that the opposite is true. "We are feeling creatures who think," she says. That's because information enters the emotional system of our brains first.

As you may remember from biology class, your brain is divided into a left and right hemisphere. Within those hemispheres, you have thinking tissue (your cerebral cortex) and emotional tissue (your limbic system). Information streams into your limbic system through your senses and then hits your amygdala—the part of your brain responsible for keeping you safe.

Your amygdala does lots of helpful things, but its most important function lies in processing fear and anxiety. When you're exposed to a dangerous situation, it immediately signals your nervous system to turn on your fight-flight-freeze response. This alarm kicks off a chain reaction of chemicals and impulses to help prepare you for combat, or to scurry, or to get really small and quiet so the (real or perceived) predator doesn't see you. (I can't tell you how many times I've wished that the Harry Potter invisibility cloak were real.)

Because your amygdala is guided by your feelings, it's able to bypass the part of your brain in charge of planning and reason. In doing so, you're able to swiftly take action without even having to think about it. In fact, your amygdala senses danger faster than any other area of your brain, which has the advantage of allowing you more time to react.

Chemicals flood your system as if preparing you for battle. Blood rushes to your arms and legs so you can punch and run. Your lungs open up so you can get more oxygen; your digestion slows so you can divert that energy elsewhere. Your heart rate increases. You become more aggressive, even surprising yourself in certain situations. And if you're like me, you pee a little (which happens when I sneeze, too, but that's another issue for another book).

Your amygdala also stores memories from your past, allowing you to form associations and beneficial behaviors in another attempt to keep you safe (aka alive). *Don't eat those berries; the last time you did you got the scoots—or worse, your cavewoman BFF croaked.*

All this is very helpful when the shit is actually hitting the fan and a real tiger is chasing you. Not so helpful in tiger-free zones like bumper-to-bumper traffic, dinner with your mother-in-law, and a stressful company meeting. Unfortunately, in today's world, our amygdalae can easily get stuck in fight, flight, or freeze mode because they have a hard time differentiating between a real tiger and a figurative one. (And there is a difference, no matter how feral your in-laws may seem.)

To make matters even more complicated, when the information coming in through your senses is unfamiliar, your brain desperately looks for data to assess the risk. But because none exists—you've never lived through a global pandemic or a war—your brain doesn't know what to do, so it throws more gasoline onto the fire, making you more anxious, out of control, and cut off from reason. That's because your brain relies on clues from the past to predict outcomes in the future. When it doesn't have enough data, it ruminates (worries and catastrophizes—on steroids).

For me, worrying is like scratching an itchy bug bite. The more I scratch, the itchier it gets. The more I worry, the more worried I become—about *everything*. Nothing helps. Not even those *X* marks you dig into your skin where the bite is.

Did I leave the stove on? The house is burning down, and the dogs are dead. *Did I leave the windows open?* The living room is flooded, and the dogs are dead. *Did I lock the doors?* There's an axe murderer waiting for me—and the dogs are dead.

SEE, I TOLD YOU SO!

But what about when our worst-case scenarios and negative fantasies come true because bad shit does happen? It can inadvertently reinforce our need to stay hypervigilant. *See, I told you so!* There was a fatal accident. Your child did die. Your partner did leave. Your best friend did lose her life to suicide. Your dad did die of cancer. Maybe if you had done more or said more, you could have helped or stopped it. In your mind you didn't do enough, so you ruthlessly beat yourself up for "failing."

While this may be hard for you to take in, no matter how bad it was or what happened, punishing yourself in perpetuity is pointless. It does no one any good, especially you. Even *if* you could have done something different, that doesn't guarantee that there would have been a different outcome. More overanalyzing or disaster dress rehearsals won't protect you or the ones you love from *everything*. We can't know the future. We're all doing the best we can with the tools we have at the time—and that includes you. Sure, it's easy to look back and think, *I shoulda, woulda, coulda done more*. But it's a waste of time, and it won't change things.

According to author and psychologist Megan Devine, "Rather than helping you feel safe, perpetual fear creates a small, hard, painful life that isn't safer than any other life. Your mind becomes an exquisite torture chamber. You can't sleep because of your anxiety, and your anxiety only gets worse because you aren't sleeping. It's an incessant hamster wheel of fears, attempts at logic, and memories of things gone wrong."

You still have life to live. Do your messiest best to move forward *with* your grief and other big emotions, *with* your awareness, *with* the knowledge you've gained in the trenches, and *with* grace for yourself and others. None of this is easy and it certainly won't erase your pain, but it can help you open the doors of the prison cell you may have put yourself in.

CARING FOR FEAR & ANXIETY

If you're anything like me, you may simply want to weed whack the crap out of these strong emotions and just be done with them. In reality, tending to them lovingly, with gentle pruning and better habits, is a far more productive and sustainable path, helping you rewire your brain, set yourself free from your unconscious (or semiconscious) addiction to fear and worry, and enjoy a bigger, fuller life.

According to psychiatrist Kristy Lamb, if we don't allow emotions like anger or grief to be felt, it's easy for them to morph into anxiety, fear, and even depression. The energy needs to go somewhere. It needs to be discharged somehow. (And if you've ever had a full-blown meltdown over something ridiculous, like a ketchup stain on your favorite sweatshirt, you know what I'm talking about.) Here are some healthy ways to channel it.

Breathe: Just the way you have a stress response (sympathetic nervous system), you also have a relaxation response (parasympathetic nervous system). When your breathing becomes rapid, shallow, or restricted, your stress response kicks in and your anxiety increases. One of the fastest ways to activate your relaxation response is through breathwork. Conscious breathing is like having a built-in stress-release valve. The easiest way to pull this valve is to make your exhalations longer than your inhalations.

Let's try it now. Inhale for four counts. Exhale for six to eight counts. Repeat this three times (or as much as needed). Our breath is central to every aspect of our well-being, yet we often overlook its power. In times of fear, grief, pain, trauma, depression, and so on, let your breath serve as the lifeline it's designed to be.

Identify what you're feeling: name it. Are your heart palpitations an indicator of fear? (They come on in a flash and have a beginning, middle, and end.) Or is it more like anxiety, worry, or rumination about something that may or may not happen? This next suggestion might sound silly, but it always helps me. Once you've identified the emotion, connect with it. "Hey, anxiety . . . Hey, sadness . . .

you're OK." Greeting and soothing our emotions reminds us that our feelings are friends, not enemies.

Validate what you're feeling: Remember, feelings aren't good or bad; they're information. They help us know how to respond in different situations. Your feelings have a right to take up space. There's nothing wrong with them or with you. They deserve to be seen without having to be fixed, justified, or controlled. They're OK, and so are you.

Soothe your inner critic: Sometimes it's hard to self-soothe when our inner critics shit all over our brains like demon-possessed parrots. You *want* to feel better, but your negative thoughts make it impossible. Inner critics are destructive for a reason: they're trying to protect us. For example, my inner critic says BS like this: *If you don't look or act a certain way, you won't be loved. You'll be left. I don't want you to experience that, so I'm going to shut you down or shame you back in line to avoid rejection.* What a sweetie pie, right? As much as we want to avoid them, inner critics need our love, because they're in a lot of pain.

A question for you to ponder as you soothe your critic: *What if the opposite of what you're feeling about yourself were true?* Think about it for a second. It's certainly possible, isn't it? Just as bad stuff can happen, so too can good stuff.

Here's another question that can help your brain get on a better track: *What would your best friend say about this?* I doubt she'd be as douchey as you (and I) can be to ourselves—because she's your best frickin' friend.

And my personal favorite: *What does love see?* Love doesn't think you're worthless, incapable, unintelligent, weak, and all the other awful things you may believe when you're out of sorts. Love sees you for who you truly are, a valuable and wonderful person. When self-attacking thoughts take hold, lean on love.

My go-to way of working through these questions is by journaling. There's just something about writing this stuff out that gives me perspective. The goal here is to give your inner critic kinder thoughts to ponder so you can take care of your feelings.

Investigate the facts: Remember, both fear and anxiety are very imaginative. The stories they tell can be over-the-top. Be a detective and look for the evidence. For example, if Neighbor Nan didn't invite you to her party, could there be a valid reason that has nothing to do with her suddenly hating you? More often than not, you won't find any shred of evidence to back up your anxiety- and fear-driven stories. And if you do find that there was some truth, it's probably nowhere close to as dire as what your imagination would have you believe.

Here's an example of how this has played out in my life: Perhaps my tumors grew a little between scans, but did they multiply like horny bunnies? No. Have they ever? No. So what's the chance they will this time? The facts after 20 years of living with cancer are pretty consistent. But in times of high stress, my imagination still needs to be reminded.

Questions for you to ponder as you investigate the facts: Do you know for certain that the scary movie you're playing in your mind will happen? Is there evidence to the contrary? Or is there someone you can call to verify facts? Could variables such as timing be in play? Or perhaps there is a more benign reason for what you've observed (for example, the tumor in my arm that turned out to not be cancerous)? And if the worst-case scenario did happen, could you handle it? How have you been able to handle difficult situations successfully in the past?

Bonus tip: Give the scary movie you're playing in your mind a funny or absurd title.

- *Woman on the Verge of a Nervous Breakdown Winds Up Fine—and Accidentally Loving Life*

- *Oops, I Farted in Yoga in Front of My New Partner and Now My Life Is Over*

- *I'm Gonna Fall Flat on My Face and Become a Social Outcast: A Musical*

Humor disarms us. It breaks the tension, creating some distance between us and the unhelpful thoughts that threaten to consume us. It can even make us smile, *God forbid.*

Get out of your head and into your body: Research shows that it's hard to solve the problems of the mind *with* the mind. When we're flooded with fear and anxiety, it's really challenging to mentally strong-arm ourselves back to calm. We need help changing our mental channel so we can choose a better path. No shame in that game.

Have you watched a dog go into brain rot—incessantly barking or licking a hot spot? Changing that behavior requires changing their physical state, perhaps getting the dog to play ball, go for a walk, or otherwise redirect their energy. Sure, you can shout "*No,* Todd!" but that doesn't always work. And even if it does, yelling only makes dogs feel more anxious. Similarly, when we're anxious, shouting "*No!*" at ourselves often makes things worse.

This is where movement comes in. Changing your physical state helps change your mental state, too. According to Dr. Wendy Suzuki, Professor of Neural Science and

Psychology at New York University, even just 10 minutes of movement per day (walking, aerobics, dance—anything you love that gets your heart pumping) significantly reduces stress and anxiety. Moving your muscles also releases what she refers to as a "bubble bath" of feel-good neurochemicals like serotonin, dopamine, and noradrenaline.

EMOTIONAL BRAVERY

It takes a lot of emotional bravery to walk this path, my friend. And though it may not feel like it now, this work will pay off in ways you can't imagine.

With that in mind, try to become more aware of the moments when you feel scared and anxious (if you're like me, that might be once or twice an hour). Instead of allowing those feelings to fester and spread, give yourself the care you deserve.

And when the going gets tough and ornery, just keep tapping into your emotional bravery—your willingness to look at what's going on with courage, curiosity, and compassion.

Remember, the more we're willing to know about ourselves, the less weird (wrong or bad) we feel. Over time we come to understand the wisdom of counterculture icon and peace activist Wavy Gravy: "We're all bozos on the bus, so might as well sit back and enjoy the ride."

CHAPTER 4

BECOMING UNBECOMING

Where there is anger, there is always pain underneath.

— ECKHART TOLLE

When I was growing up, my grandma taught me that certain behaviors were "unbecoming" for women.

"Be nice. Sit like a lady. Don't cry. Stop being so vulgar."

Fearing her reprimand, I didn't fart until my mid-40s, which was when I realized I had free will. Ever the survivor, Grandma wanted me to fit into a world that wasn't built for me. In her well-meaning eyes, unbecoming behavior would hinder my chance of eventually attracting a respectable husband—her ultimate goal for me.

Like many women of her time, she was taught to contain herself in order to fit in. To quiet down, be polite, and not ruffle feathers. That didn't mean that she didn't feel the full range of human emotions; she just learned to hide or express them in different ways.

For all her best efforts, she failed to instill these antiquated ideas of femininity in me. I stink at hiding things. I'm not a quiet person. I don't want to be polite when it's not warranted. I like ruffling feathers when I see or experience injustice or when I'm walking down the street and a male stranger tells me, "Smile, you're so much prettier that way." And lying? I'm terrible at it. Do not commit a crime with me. We will get caught.

According to Soraya Chemaly, writer and social activist, women in particular are more likely to stuff their anger down than to express it. We're socialized to use minimizing language, keep the peace, and be deferential. But no one can be an emotional shock absorber forever. Denying our stronger emotions is likely one of the reasons our bodies break down and get sick.

Men don't exactly have a cake walk when it comes to expressing themselves, either. They're commonly punished for behaviors and emotions that are deemed too feminine. Fear, sadness, or anything considered "weak." On the flip side, they're often praised for showing emotions associated with masculinity, regardless of whether it's toxic or not. Think: staying stoic in the face of deep pain, hauling off and hitting someone to "defend" their honor, or needing to be overly independent, as if asking for help (or directions!) is a sin. It's a hot mess, y'all!

Without question, anger was at the very top of Grandma's "unbecoming" list. Anger is another taboo, especially misunderstood and vilified for women. But according to psychologist and anger researcher Dr. Ryan Martin, it's *good* that we feel angry. When bad things happen, we hurt deeply. When we witness or experience injustice, anger is appropriate, *damn it!*

The more I researched anger, the more I realized how pervasive it was. Our culture is riddled with rage. (Case in point: any online comment section on the Internet.) And yet, like grief, we don't talk about it. Instead, we're quick to point fingers, get outraged, and find fault with others. We're afraid to look at our own anger.

Research from the University of California–Berkeley illustrates that we usually learn how to experience and deal with anger from our families of origin. In some families, emotions are expressed regardless of the consequences, while other families can't tolerate any show of emotion at all. Some members may be allowed to express certain emotions, while others aren't. Double standards like these only heap on the resentment and generate more dysfunction. No wonder we've got trunks of baggage to unpack.

Anger is especially common in the face of loss. We act out instead of crying out, because anger feels powerful, while grief feels powerless. Until I started doing this work, I had no idea how intertwined my grief and anger had become. I'd stuff, suppress, and contain my feelings until they migrated and mutated beyond my control. All that energy had to go somewhere. What follows are the messy stories of where it went.

THE GOLDEN YEARS ARE FOR SHIT

In the last year or so of his life, Dad began dropping wisdom bombs. Big life lessons like "Always keep the promises you make to yourself," or "Tell people you love them. If you feel it, say it, because life is too precious to hold back."

I never knew when a nugget was coming, so I kept a notes doc on my phone to capture each word, typing with a mixture of inspiration and desperation, not wanting to forget even a syllable. In the beginning, he weaved these bombs into relevant conversations, which made them easier to process. But as his time grew shorter, the bombs became more frequent, more urgent, and definitely more unexpected, totally catching me off guard.

Naturally, these bombs could set off a chain reaction of feelings I had been trying to quell. But the last thing I wanted was to burst into tears at the mere suggestion that I "consider a car trade-in after 50,000 miles." I mean, maybe the guy just wanted to talk about cars. No big life lessons. No trying to squeeze in as much fatherly advice while he still could—just cars (and common sense). Next thing he knows, he's comforting a hysterical daughter, when *he* is the one who needs comforting in the form of a normal conversation that has nothing to do with dying.

I'd get so angry with myself for my inability to contain my emotions, especially if my waterworks were triggered by something as harmless as a TV commercial (unless it was for the ASPCA and featured a senior collie named Wags who desperately needed a home—those are impossible to survive without tears streaming down your face).

One such occasion was when my parents came to our home for a visit. As I was helping Dad bring their luggage upstairs to our guest room, he paused to catch his breath and drop a wisdom bomb while he was at it.

"You know, love, sometimes the golden years are for shit."

Oh sweet Jesus, here we go.

"Look at this bag," he said, pointing to a small suitcase. "You know what's in it? Medications! This entire bag is filled with our pills. Everyone works so hard so things can be better *later*, but we've got it all backward. You have to live your life *now*, love. Make *now* your golden years. Slow down and give yourself more of the good stuff along the way. Sometimes I worry that you're following in my footsteps and missing too many of the moments that matter."

His words hit me hard. Not only could I feel his regret, but there was a reason he was saying this to me. As one of the few people who really knew how I was wired, he was highlighting the code I hadn't yet cracked, the one I was uncomfortable discussing, even with him. There was only one way to respond.

DEAD MOUSE!

That's right. When a sudden onset of feelings triggers a tidal wave of overwhelm, sadness, or regret, one of the ways I dam them up is by conjuring awful images in my mind, stuff like eating anchovies or, say, a dead mouse in my sink. (It's a useful technique. You're welcome.)

Dead mouse, dead mouse, dead mouse! . . . Distraction created, crisis averted. At least temporarily.

While my mind games may seem odd, we humans are wired weird for good reason. In psychology, there's a theory known as *mortality salience*. It suggests that when our evolutionary drive to survive collides with our inevitable realization that we will all eventually die, we freak the fuck out. Terror ensues. And because terror is, well, terrifying, we develop clever ways to distract ourselves from it. There are millions of ways to divert attention from this terror—buy a midlife-crisis sports car, get your helicopter mom pilot's license, hoover all the Ho Hos in a three-state radius, the list goes on and on. But my tried-and-true diversion remains two syllables long: *Dead mouse!*

TICK. TICK. BOOM!

In October of 2018, Dad's cancer returned, and technically, it wasn't a recurrence; it was a new diagnosis of pancreatic cancer—as if lightning had struck twice in the same frickin' place. Within days, he was back at the hospital for another surgery, followed a few months later by more chemo. By that summer, the cancer would spread to his liver, and he would be told that his disease had become terminal.

"I really thought I'd be one of the 10 percent who makes it," he shared, as he began to wrap his mind around what that actually meant, since curing was no longer an option. Suddenly, Dad found himself walking the precarious line between living fully and actively dying, between making the most of the time he had left and simultaneously winding it all down. As this new phase set in, Dad's behavior might not have looked different to our extended circle of family and friends, but I noticed the changes. He paused longer in conversations, smiling in wonder and awe as if he were standing on the edge of the Grand Canyon, taking in the majesty of it all while he still could.

Mom and I helped him create a bucket list, and I took it upon myself to be our event planner. (The recovering perfectionist in me was thrilled at the opportunity to relapse.) Dad wanted to go to Lake Placid in the Adirondacks one more time, to sit at the water's edge and do jigsaw puzzles by the fire. To visit his brother in Cape Cod and reminisce about the old days "and have a few good chuckles." And to celebrate his 72nd birthday on Martha's Vineyard and my 48th "somewhere nice."

We set out to make as many memories as possible and as quickly as possible, trip by trip. That summer was "brutiful," as Glennon Doyle would say, both beautiful and brutal.

First stop: his birthday celebration in Martha's Vineyard. This idyllic little island off the coast of Massachusetts is known for its quaint harbor towns, sandy beaches, postcard-worthy lighthouses, and lush farmland. My perfectionist was pleased. For years, Dad had casually talked about visiting the island, and we all thought that sounded lovely, but we'd never gotten around to it. Now, all our rain checks were being cashed in, all at once.

We arrived a few days early to take in the sights. Mom and I wandered among the charming shops, while Dad and Brian sat outside on nearby benches, reading the local paper and shooting the breeze. We drank delicious afternoon coffees and early-evening cocktails. Roamed the wild coastline and collected shells on our walks to remember our visit.

At times, it felt as if we were being given a reprieve from our worries. From being full-time patients and caregivers, to just being a normal family again. For a brief moment I even allowed myself to believe that the Vineyard might possess special powers, like a Bermuda Triangle of sorts. But instead of planes disappearing in the vortex, it made tumors vanish.

Unfortunately, later that night, as Dad and I sat on the deck outside the rental house sipping our gin and tonics and watching as the sky turn orange-pink, cancer once again infiltrated. And when it did, I could feel the weight of the world bearing down on his shoulders.

"What's on your mind, Dad?" I gently asked.

"I'm setting goals to help me hang on as long as I can," he responded. "A small Super Bowl party with my friends this winter, a new car for Mom, great little trips like this with you guys. But I don't know how many goals to make. I'm just not ready to go yet." Tears gathered in his sunken eyes.

Change the subject. Lighten the mood. Be reassuring. I quickly searched for what to say or do to help him feel even the slightest bit better. My mind flashed to all the times he'd comforted me. He always had the right words at the right time.

"I'm not ready for you to go yet, either, Dad, and I'm so sorry we can't fix what we desperately want to fix. This really sucks," I said, reaching for his hand. "But let's make life a little easier where we can. . . . How are your symptoms today?" I was referring to the little hemorrhoidal bastards that had flared during our trip. His gut was ravaged by treatments, and while I was helpless against his mortality, hemorrhoids gave me something to do.

"Well, they suck, too," he replied with a hint of laughter.

"*That* I can fix, Dad! I'm heading to CVS to get a sitz bath and some Epsom salt. Let's at least get you some relief downtown," I said with a wink.

"I love that I can talk about anything with you, Kristin," he said.

"Me, too, Dad," I said reflexively. When I thought about it, though, I wasn't sure if it was true.

In order to really be able to talk about "anything," I'd have to learn how to talk about dying. Why was this so hard? I bought books on Buddhism, listened to the meditations, took the classes, and hired the professionals. But nothing prepared me for this. We learn so many important skills for navigating life. Essential hygiene practices: check. Don't take rides from strangers: check. How to use jumper cables: check (or just call AAA). Supporting someone we love through their last breath: crickets.

Even with all the preparation in the world—even when we think we know what we're doing—practicing it is a whole other skill. Dad had opened a big door, one he needed to explore, but I wasn't capable of accompanying him through it yet, so I hid behind anal prolapses as an escape from my own discomfort.

The next night, we celebrated his birthday at a beautiful restaurant with a gorgeous view of the water. The air was warm, salty, and slightly breezy—the temperature just right. The ocean shimmered like a Monet painting sparkling with magic-hour light. Even our table was the best in the house (I made sure of it, as I didn't want to leave anything to chance).

Dad ordered a great bottle of wine, as he always did. Brian, my normally stoic husband, was tasked with kicking off the birthday toast. One sentence in, his lips began quivering, unleashing a chain reaction of feels that rippled throughout the table. Mom's eyes welled up. I retreated to my mental safe house—*What would it be like to be the ocean?* I wondered, as I willed my tears away with thoughts. *Something that endures and remains no matter how life changes.*

But I wasn't the ocean; I was a hurting human, surrounded by other hurting humans who didn't know how to express their big feelings, let alone realize that it might be appropriate.

Just then Dad swooped in to save us, allowing us to breathe again.

"Thank you for coming here to celebrate this special day with me," he said, gazing at the ocean I was trying to become. "You know, if I could do it all again, I'd give myself more like this. Summer has always been my busy season. And even though I could have, I rarely took a day off to experience something like this. So figure out what your 'more like this' looks like and make it happen sooner; don't save it for your golden years."

Before I had a chance to let his words sink in, words that would become my compass in this next stage of life, he lobbed the final bomb that demolished my brittle defenses. "I hope you'll all come back here on my birthday from time to time. This is a good spot to remember me. I love you all."

Mom leaned over and kissed him on the cheek. Brian nodded and said, "Love you." Meanwhile, I was not having it. I excused myself to the bathroom with some faux-upbeat comment like, "Jeez, Dad. Now I need to go fix my mascara—be right back."

Hot tears breached the surface as I briskly searched for the ladies' room. I begged them to stop—*Please, not now!*—but my ducts overrode the system. No nail digging. No anchovies. No dead mice. No mental decoys or emotional jiujitsu could hold back my tidal wave of emotions from finally breaking.

Once I found the bathroom, I locked the door behind me and promptly fell to pieces. Grief poured out of all the nooks and crannies I'd ergonomically stuffed it in. *Come back to Martha's Vineyard on his birthday without him? No way, no how.* That would mean there was a world in which he didn't exist. I couldn't handle that.

Flashes of all the things I was going to miss doing with Dad rotated through my brain. Searching for treasures at the flea market on Sundays, phone calls to tell him about my latest creative endeavor, needling each other on election nights with playful text threads, hikes with our dogs, sunset boat rides on the lake where my parents lived for over 30 years in their dream house.

The ordinary pleasures that make up an extraordinary life. Experiences I would no longer have after he left me. . . .

Shit. There it was, the heart of the pain I'd worked so hard to heal or avoid—abandonment.

Once again, I would be fatherless.

Through my desperate gasps, I heard what sounded like a moan. Was there someone else waiting to restuff their pain in the privacy of a dark ladies' room? After a disorienting moment, I soon realized the moans were coming from me. I'd never made sounds like this before—foreign, guttural, primal. They were the sounds of agony.

The real, kind, and stable Dad I'd prayed for, to both Jesus and Santa (to cover my bases), the one who was present and loving, the one who accepted me for who I was, not who he expected me to be, the one who *stayed*—I'd finally found him, and now cancer, the very thing I'd worked so damn hard to accept and cohabitate with, was taking him from me.

Suddenly, I was furious with myself, my disease, and the entire world.

Fuck you, cancer! I hate you!

Stop it, Kris. Don't ruin his birthday with your hysterics. Pull yourself together.

I ran the sink and submerged my hands in ice-cold water to shock my system back into submission. Still no composure. I prayed to the God who had clearly forgotten me, but that only made me wail more. I tried deep breathing. The air refused to fill my lungs. With each sob, I felt like I was being ripped apart from seam to seam. Something had to save me before total annihilation.

That's when rage kicked in.

Before I knew what hit me, my hand was slapping my face. *What the hell are you doing?* Finally, the pain from my stinging cheeks overtook the anguish in my heart. At last, relief.

Field note from grief: always carry a good tube of concealer and some powder. You'll need it.

I fixed my makeup and returned to the table. Shocked, stunned, but pulled together. I acted like nothing happened. I made light conversation. *How good is this lightly floured zucchini blossom?* I laughed when appropriate and drank wine (but not too much, fearing I might lose it again). Despite the disturbing interlude of self-abuse, I even enjoyed much of the remaining evening. Grandma wouldn't have approved of my methods, but at least she'd give me points for carrying cover-up and getting on with a grand old time.

A COCKTAIL OF SHAME

The next morning I woke up with a big AR (agonizing reappraisal) hangover. Even though I was the only one who witnessed my unhinged spectacle, I was sick with shame.

Why couldn't I be the type of person who didn't do insane things like that? Instead, I felt like Annette Bening's character in the film *American Beauty*. A positive-thinking, obsessed Realtor who breaks down in a self-slapping fit when she fails to sell a house. "You big baby! Stop it!" she screams, before collecting herself and silently walking out. But like Annette's character, this house was my everything, too.

At least no one saw me, I thought. *I can keep this pathetic meltdown to myself.* Lock it up. Throw away the key. Smile. Yeah, right. Who was I kidding?

A few weeks later, our Bucket List Tour brought us all to Newport, to celebrate my birthday. By this time, I really thought I could keep a lid on any outbursts. I'd talked about it in therapy. Did a bunch of energy work, yada yada. In my mind, I was all set.

After a lovely dinner (with no interludes), I was standing outside the restaurant waiting for the valet to bring the car around. My parents were using the restroom; Brian was searching through his pockets for a tip. *I'm so grateful we're here together,* I thought. *And bonus points for not losing my shit.* Clearly, I believed I was growing.

Not so fast, Speed Racer.

As the car pulled up, three drunk dudes tumbled out of the lobby. One guy put his hand on my shoulder and said/slurred, "You're pretty, come to a bar with us." Another crawled into the back seat of our car. I lost track of the third one. He was probably puking in the bushes.

"Not gonna happen," I replied as I removed his grabby hand from my shoulder, before turning to his friend. "Hey, buddy. This isn't an Uber. Please get out of our car." He stared at me defiantly, while rifling through our things.

It all happened so fast, it was disorienting. Though Brian was nearby talking to the attendant, he hadn't registered what was going on yet.

Not willing to take no for an answer, Grabby Hands made another attempt. This time leaning in closer. "Come on, baby, don't be so lame. Have some fun with us."

"Dude! Back off. I'm *not* interested. And get your friend *out* of our car!"

"Oh, fuck you, cunt," he said, his tone suddenly turning dangerous. "You're not even worth it—you're just all that's left."

Oopsy. . . .

My brain went offline. All my unbecoming emotions gathered force, ready for battle. No, not ready—salivating. Longing to fight for every time I'd been demeaned, harassed, or assaulted. The stalker who terrorized me, the repairman who shoved his tongue down my throat, the date that turned dangerous the minute I entered his apartment, the stranger sitting next to me on the train. Glaring at me. Masturbating. Using my book to tidy up when he was finished. All the ways I had to abdicate my personal boundaries—to be quiet, clever, and just "take it"—to survive. I was used to those bad behaviors; many women are. How utterly audacious of me to indicate I'd had enough.

"You have no idea what a *cunt* I can be, you drunk fuck, but you're about to find out!" I screamed, followed by a deluge of more (very loud) and unbecoming expletives.

By now, Brian was well aware of what was happening. Within seconds he'd separated me from the men, who were each bigger than the both of us combined. Security rushed in, demanding they leave the property. The hotel felt so bad that they gave us a free night. A courteous gesture, but it wasn't enough. I wanted something I couldn't have: moral fairness—as if that even exists.

Those jackasses would get to keep living their sloppy, entitled lives, freely harassing women with no consequences. But my dad would be lucky if he lived another season? *Bullshit!*

Under the light of unfairness, my rage made absolute sense to me. That is, until I turned and saw Dad standing there in shock. Helpless, rattled—fragile. If one of those guys had mistakenly stumbled into him, it could have put him in the hospital, again. Looking at how vulnerable and upset he was, every cell of my being flooded with shame.

Shame is one of those emotions that should come with a big roll of yellow caution tape. Through Brené Brown's research on the subject, I've learned that shame is the intensely painful feeling or experience of believing that we're flawed and unworthy of love, belonging, and connection. Shame is a focus on self. While guilt is a focus on behavior. Shame is "I am bad." Guilt is "I did something bad."

My shame hangover—there was no Excedrin for this one—was partly due to the fact that I had allowed my anger to erupt in unconstructive ways. Yes, I wish I had made different choices earlier on in that bathroom and with Grabby Hands, but I tried to look on the bright side: at least my therapist got some great new material to work with. But what rattled me was my complete and utter lack of control. I'd been desperately trying to make Dad think I was OK, that he didn't have to worry about me. He could trust me to be responsible when he was gone. I'd take care of things like he taught me. I'd be steady. Unrattled. Holding fast.

While I hesitated to share these "unbecoming stories," they are real examples of what the "fight" response can look like in grief. They're not pretty, but they're also nothing to be ashamed of. Instead, they're more examples of why it's so important to understand the many shapes and sizes of our feelings and how they work together.

THE UPSIDE AND DOWNSIDE OF ANGER

Now that I got all that gunk out (phew!), let's take a step back and get to know the so-called monster: anger. What it is, why we have it, why it isn't all bad, and how we can respect and better channel it. Because here's the sitch: You better believe that when your world falls apart, there's a good chance that you're going to be angry—and rightly so. But as I've learned, it's better to care for our anger than to allow it to simmer, seethe, and spew.

Anger is an instinctive response to a perceived threat, violation, or injustice. It isn't a character defect to avoid. It's a blinking red light telling us that something is *not* OK.

Anger's job is to protect us at all costs. It does that in obvious and not-so-obvious ways. We're more familiar with the obvious ways—tick, tick, *boom!* It's the covert stuff that can sideswipe us. For example, anger can shield us from feelings that feel way too big and scary to accept or tend to. *Don't worry,* anger says. *I got this.*

And while some folks are quick to anger, others may have a hard time even identifying that they're angry at all. You're likely familiar with those seemingly gentle creatures. Everyone knows they're angry but them. Or no one knows they're angry until they have either a heart attack or a playdate with an axe.

Regardless of how anger manifests, it's always trying to protect us—even from itself.

Anger affects you physically, too. Your heart rate speeds up, you sweat, a surge of adrenaline blasts through your body, your face turns red, your jaw clenches—readying to defend. Then, once the real or perceived threat passes, there's a physiological wind-down period. If you've ever been steaming mad, you know that it's near impossible to chill out right away. It takes time to calm down all that powerful energy.

In fact, it's difficult to relax and restore our nervous systems after an angry episode. That's because the adrenaline surge, and all that comes with it, can last for hours, even days, past the episode. And because all those chemicals remain pumped up in our bodies, wreaking havoc on our nervous systems, we're more likely to experience continued anger.

CHECK YOURSELF BEFORE YOU WRECK YOURSELF

So, we've clearly established that our anger is valid, important, and there for a reason. But that doesn't absolve us when it's destructive or misdirected. Or when we use it as a decoy to avoid responsibility for what is actually our side of the street. Instead of addressing the underlying reason for the unrest, the focus goes squarely on the shoulders of the anger that was expressed—as if *that's* the real problem.

While anger can be helpful in certain situations, like motivating us to change things that aren't working, we don't want to do what Thich Nhat Hanh, Buddhist monk and peace activist, calls "training in aggression" or "rehearsing our anger," which only cements unhelpful patterns of holding on to anger. When left unchecked, anger isolates us, injures our relationships, hurts others, and damages our physical and mental health, making us more prone to chronic inflammation, depression, heart attacks, stroke, and even cancer.

Again, anger in and of itself isn't the problem. It's how we cope with it that matters. Just as we don't want to let our resentments drive the bus, we don't want to suppress or neglect our anger, either. That would be another example of abandoning our own needs.

Remember, anger is especially common and appropriate in the face of all kinds of loss, including betrayal, divorce, and death. If you're feeling it, welcome to the party. *The mocktails are on the table in the back. No vodka. Too dangerous.* Again, we act out instead of crying out because anger feels powerful, while grief feels powerless. That's why some of us have an easier time turning to anger instead of grief. In essence, that's what anger is trying to communicate: *"Ow! This hurts!"*

Other times, we point our anger in directions that don't deserve our wrath. Our rational minds understand that we're not to blame for what happened, and yet we're angry at ourselves for not doing more. Or we're angry at the person for not taking better care of themselves. Angry they chose to drive down that street the day of the accident. Angry we didn't drive instead. Angry at other family members for not showing up. Meanwhile, they've got their own traumas and dramas that have nothing to do with us, yet we take their absence personally. Angry at God for not protecting us. If he, she, it can't keep us safe, how the heck are we supposed to trust life or anyone in it?

Simply put, when it comes to anger, there's often more than meets the eye.

THE ANGER ICEBERG

Another reason anger is such a powerful emotion is that it rarely shows up alone. Instead, it's usually accompanied by other emotions that you may not know how to access or express, or think you have a right to feel, like grief, guilt, shame, embarrassment, anxiety, loneliness, hopelessness, or a combination thereof.

Researchers from the Gottman Institute say that it can be helpful to think of anger like an iceberg. With icebergs, the tip may look like a large mass, but in reality it's only a small part that we see. Most of the iceberg is actually hidden below the water. This is how anger can work, too.

In fact, anger is commonly referred to as a secondary or "indicator" emotion. It steps in and points out a whole host of other big and raw emotions roiling under the surface.

For example, let's say you're annoyed that you have to go to a friend's baby shower. Having had a miscarriage yourself, the last thing you want is to be around cute babies or happy mothers. You're envious your friend got pregnant so easily, when it's been so hard and painful for you to conceive. These complicated feelings are completely justified. They don't make you a jerk; they make you a normal, hurting human. I'll be honest, if I had to watch a father-daughter dance at a wedding after Dad passed, I'd have tossed a banana peel on the floor and prayed for a full-on wipeout (and pileup).

Anger indicates that there's more to the story than meets the eye. It asks us to be courageous and go deeper. To explore the pain beneath the outrage. The heartbreak, rejection, sadness, fear, betrayal, and so on. Our anger never needs to be justified to make sense. Your pain, like mine, isn't looking for validation; it just wants permission to exist.

Now, we may not always be able to identify the whole emotional enchilada right away. It's easy to go from zero to 60 without realizing what else is at work. But as we become more skilled at approaching our anger with curiosity, compassion, and care, instead of feeling shame, we're better able to regulate our emotions and less likely to lash out at ourselves and others.

CARING FOR YOUR ANGER

When it comes to defusing red-hot rage, the goal is to quell the fire and calm your nervous system. Below are many suggestions, but you don't have to try them all or apply them in any particular sequence. You'll also notice that some suggestions overlap with tips from other chapters—that's because the methods for restoring your nervous system are very similar.

Breathe: Anger tells your brain that you're in crisis. Breathwork reminds you that right now, in this moment, you are safe. We explored the power of elongating your exhale in the last chapter. My next favorite exercise is called box breathing. Give it a try now. Inhale through your nose for four counts. Hold your breath for four counts. Exhale through your mouth for four counts. Hold your breath for four counts. Repeat this three times or as many as needed. As you do this, you'll literally begin to feel yourself moving out of your stress response (fight, flight, freeze) and into your relaxation response (rest and digest).

Allow yourself to feel your anger: Identify that what you're feeling is actually anger. Call it out: "I am angry." If expressing anger is hard for you, this might be difficult at first. But you are not expected to gloss over your angry feelings with positivity. Get down with what's coming up. Where is it located in your body? Your throat or chest? Breathe into those areas and allow them to release.

Investigate your trigger: What set you off? *Loud chewing! Slow drivers! Rude people!* I get it; that stuff ticks me off, too. But it's not the full story. What's going on under the surface? *I feel out of control. Ignored. Unimportant.* Or maybe you were reminded of an earlier experience in your life that was unfair. Anger always contains important messages for your growth. Understanding your triggers can help you stay grounded.

Explore your pre-anger state: Your mood before the incident occurred can also play a role in how you responded. When I'm hungry, I'm far less patient. *Get that girl a sandwich,* *stat!* Perhaps you tipped back one too many Manhattans the night before. Maybe you were already riled up about something else, or you were just having a pressure-filled day. Understanding the context can help you care for your anger going forward.

Identify your "do differently's": So you snapped. Shit happens. How do you want to respond differently next time? What kind of support do you need for that to happen? Sometimes it's therapy; other times it could be a day off, a good cry, a much-needed infusion of *joy.* It's easy to get pissed off when you're in a joy famine or you've been ignoring your own needs for too long. Don't shoot the messenger, but in these cases, you're probably most angry with yourself.

Journal it out: Get your tumultuous thoughts out of your head and onto a piece of paper. What happened? How did it make you feel? What other feelings came up? How did you respond? How could you have responded instead? What will you do now to feel better? What can you do next time to avoid being in this situation or a situation like this? (Because, believe me, there *will* be a next time.) Freewrite whatever comes to mind. Too afraid someone will see your deepest, darkest thoughts? Lock them up. Put barbed wire around them. Set a solid boundary: "Don't read my shit!"

Channel your fury: Give your anger something constructive to do—a job, a project, a workout, an artistic outlet. Channel that energy into something that makes a positive difference. Protest. Volunteer. Donate. Write. Sing. Move. Make art. Basically, choose a healthy action to help move your big, intense feelings through and out of your body.

Say you're sorry: Sometimes our anger is 100 percent appropriate. Other times, we've messed up. If you made a mistake, or hurt someone, own up to it—without caveats. *Sorry for calling you a dirtbag, but you were being a dirtbag.* Nope. That's not it. When you recognize that you were out of line, just say you're sorry, full stop.

Forgive yourself: Don't beat yourself up, pal. It's over. Let yourself off the hook. Give yourself the grace to move on, knowing that by being accountable you've acted with integrity. You're doing the best you can during a shitty time. None of this is easy, but this work can actually make your relationships stronger.

YOU'VE GOT THIS

This is big stuff, and I'm superproud of you/us for exploring it. And guess what? You don't have to continue this on your own. Work with a therapist, ask for help from a trusted friend, join a support group. There are so many outlets available to us now.

Above all, make a promise to yourself (repeat after me):
I will not punish myself for my feelings.
I will release myself from torturing myself over past behaviors.
I will remember that I am doing the best I can.
I will move forward with love.

Anger is healthy. If it wasn't for anger, many of the freedoms we hold dear wouldn't exist. Remember, when we have the courage to explore our unbecoming feelings, a world of healing opens up to us. We experience better health, deeper intimacy, and stronger connections, which opens the door to a whole lot more love.

CHAPTER 5

GRIEF & TRAUMA

The Golden Repair

Grief, I've learned, is really just love. It's all the love you
want to give, but cannot. All that unspent love gathers
up in the corners of your eyes, the lump in your throat,
and in that hollow part of your chest. Grief is just love
with no place to go.

— JAMIE ANDERSON

There's an ancient Japanese art of repairing broken
objects that holds helpful lessons we can apply to our
hearts. This centuries-old practice is called *kintsukuroi*,
which translates to "golden repair." When pottery breaks,
instead of being thrown out, the piece is lovingly repaired
with gold leaf hand-painted over every crack and crevice.
As a result, what was damaged becomes unique and more
beautiful—"a conversation piece," as my grandma would

say. Something with new life, precious history, a symbol of honor and reverence for life's inevitable fractures.

We, too, are more beautiful as a result of our once-broken, now-mended parts. And whatever caused the crack—such as neglect, betrayal, abuse, trauma, loss, or death—the process of repair begins with grieving. Allowing ourselves to feel is the gold that makes us whole again.

A few weeks after my dad was diagnosed, the best thing I did for myself was to get my ass back into therapy. I've been on and off the couch since I was a teenager. Back then, I was forced to go. Given my situation with bio dad and other ruptures, my mom thought I had a lot to "process" (which was spot-on), so she sent me to Dr. Ronald once a week during high school.

When other teenagers were hanging out, flirting, studying, or sneaking cigarettes behind the gym, I was staging a silent protest in Dr. Ron's office, refusing to utter a word. What can I say? I had a rebellious streak and wanted to thwart my parents' ability to get their money's worth. Oh, the wisdom of youth.

Over the years, I've had many great therapists (and a few duds). So when the floor dropped out from under me, again, that's when Carole came into the picture.

Carole, I should mention, is both wise and hilarious. She has witty sayings that go deep, making me laugh and think. I call them Carole-isms (delivered in her classic New York accent). Stuff like:

- "If it's not one thing, it's your mother."

- "Looks like you're experiencing an AFGO (another fucking growth opportunity)."

- "If it's hysterical, it's historical."

And the one I'm learning most about in this season of life: "When the grief train pulls into the station, it brings all the other cars with it."

Grief doesn't occur in isolation. One loss brings up past losses, even ones we may think we're "over." Whether we're conscious of it or not, we're not grieving just the present loss but other losses that came before it. No wonder grief is so scary and exhausting. It rips us open, dislodging a backlog of old grief in the process. Together, the old aches and fresh despair feel like a tsunami of emotions that will drain our very life force if we don't protect ourselves.

But there's no real protection from painful feelings, and as we've been exploring, the act of holding them back is equally painful and draining. It also takes an enormous amount of work—energy that's far better spent healing rather than resisting. Plus, as the *Star Trek* wisdom goes, "resistance is futile." One way or another, the waves of pain will eventually hit you. Managing those waves one at a time is far easier.

Grief isn't just about death, either. The litany of losses we each face in a lifetime is too numerous to count. We endure abuse. Friendships end. We get divorced, lose our jobs and identities. We'll lose our connection to self and wonder why we're even here in the first place. We become chronically or gravely ill—even when we do our best not to. We mess up in unimaginable ways because unimaginable things happen to us. The shades of loss are many, and we need to mourn it all—big and small.

The point is, no one gets out of life scratch-free or stain resistant. If we're lucky enough to be alive, good times and bad times are inevitable. Expecting *only* the good times makes us emotionally unprepared for the ever-changing, uncertain nature of life. And as Carole, my therapist, would say, "It is what it is, and you don't have to like it." Fantastic! I don't.

But in our perfection-driven and grief-phobic society, few of us are taught how to respond to loss. Instead, we're taught how to avoid pain. The thing that makes it such a big, unwieldy emotion is that, similar to anger, grief encapsulates so many other emotions, too (anxiety, guilt, rage, shame—basically a bunch of the "unbecoming" stuff). We don't avoid grief just because it's grief; we avoid it because of *everything* associated with it—the hysterical, the historical, and the downright horrifying.

Believe it or not, this avoidance is as natural as the sun rising. We're biologically wired to behave this way. From an evolutionary perspective, part of our development was to learn which situations to avoid in order to survive—stuff like poisonous berries and venomous snakes, but also emotional pain (danger) and isolation (exile from the community we needed to stay alive). So there's a part of this behavior that comes from an essential place: survival.

Avoidance has another jagged silver lining, beyond primal instincts: burying the source of our suffering in chaos often creates dramatic fires that feel easier to extinguish. That way, we can channel our pain into situational soap operas that, weirdly, also serve us. Think Julianne Moore in the movie *Magnolia*. She loses her shit on the pharmacist who calls her "lady" when what's really going on is she's desperately struggling with her father's terminal illness (sounds familiar). Distraction or projection as avoidance seemingly gives us a free pass so that we don't have to go into the deep, dark places and risk acknowledging just how thoroughly and completely our hearts are shattered.

But that acknowledgment will come anyway—often manifesting itself within our bodies. We don't even have to be in a full-blown grief-a-palooza to experience visceral symptoms of loss. Depression. Anxiety. Appetite loss or gain. Digestive issues. Fatigue. Malaise. Lower immunity, aches, pains, inflammation, insomnia or too much sleep, heart issues, and so on.

We vacillate between nausea and ravenousness. Normal things like going to the grocery store can be totally over-whelming. Showering is an award-worthy achievement. What's left of our memory goes on the fritz. Before grief, I'd sometimes forget where I put my car keys; now I forget what the car that I've owned for 12 years even looks like.

As Elizabeth Gilbert so beautifully says:

> Grief carves you out—it comes in the mid-dle of the night, comes in the middle of the day, comes in the middle of a meeting, comes in the middle of a meal. It *arrives*—it's this tremendously forceful arrival and it cannot be resisted without you suffering more. . . . The posture that you take is you hit your knees in absolute humility and you let it rock you until it is done with you. And it will be done with you, eventually. And when it is done, it will leave. But to stiffen, to resist, and to fight it is to hurt yourself.

Yet despite these concrete experiences of emotional and physical pain, avoidance remains a favorite coping mechanism. As a result, grief winds up being very, very lonely. The need to avoid our pain can lead to isolating ourselves from loved ones. For some, this may mean isolat-ing from romantic partners, withdrawing physically and sexually, which pulls us further away from healing touch, oftentimes creating hurt and resentment in the other person—especially if they're also grieving. When we're struggling to understand our feelings, we may act out in insensitive ways, creating more distance in the relationship. I wish there were a Hallmark card for those cringey moments: *Remember when I told you to "Fuck off"? Grief had the mic. I'm so sorry!*

At work, grief can play out when we get overwhelmed easily and are unable to focus. When we feel out of control, we might fly off the handle and snap at a co-worker for asking an innocent question like, "Are you going to be on today's call?" or "Do you want a veggie burger or a slice of pizza?" Or maybe we vanish from normal water-cooler chatter and other social niceties because the only way we know how to lick our wounds is to retreat, like a wounded animal.

Bottom line: neglected grief will do whatever it must to let all that big, emotional energy out, morphing into unpredictable rage, anxiety, hypervigilance, hyperdrive, procrastination, and addictions that offer temporary comfort in the storm. But, as noted, it can go even further, like when unprocessed grief shows up as unfinished business, following us around, negatively impacting our lives until we're brave enough to tend to it.

RETURN TO BROKEN ROAD

In 2021, I began to delve into some of the other cars my grief train brought with it. Like, for example, the unprocessed grief over the fact that, for the past 20 years, my body has shared space with dozens of tumors. As a veteran stage IV cancer thriver (again, someone who lives with cancer—it's not gone, neat, or tidy), I genuinely thought I'd already processed the grief of my diagnosis and how it changed my life forever. I thought I was done.

In retrospect, I have to laugh, because it's funny to think I could scratch off grief like the silvery coating on a lottery ticket. My grief over Dad's illness brought up all that old, hidden pain. It showed me how at the center of our grief can be unresolved traumas—big and small. In fact, grief and trauma often go hand in hand. In trauma there is loss of some kind. Loss of safety, security, love, trust, innocence. For some of us, it can come as a surprise that when we're ready to sit with our grief, the traumatized parts of us come up for healing, too—at long last.

Given my history with my bio dad, it shouldn't have come as such a surprise. The first time I met him in person, plenty of old emotions came rushing back—and they didn't stop with that panic attack I had in my dad's car. You may recall that I'd been terrified of losing control, and in retrospect, I can see that was a "grief car" moment (fitting that it happened in Dad's gray Buick). All the times I'd felt lonely, abandoned, or enraged threatened to overwhelm me.

I'll never forget opening the door of the car and glancing up as my bio dad came out of his house to greet us. My heart was beating out of my chest as we walked toward each other. I was too scared to lift my head and search for anything more than brief glimpses of him. But when I did, it was like looking into a mirror. There before me was my nose, my green eyes, my forehead. My legs, lips, and shyness. Seeing myself in him and him in me made me feel happy and sad at the same time. Happy I finally had answers. Sad I'd spent nearly two decades wondering what his deal was and taking his rejection personally. *Keep it together, you can do this.*

"Hi, I'm Crispin," he said, raising his hand to shake mine.

"Hi, I'm Kristin," I replied, raising my hand to meet his.

I remember only snippets from the rest of that weekend. Sailing on his boat. A walk in the woods. Finding a clamshell on the beach (that sits in my bathroom with a candle in it to this day). Telling him I wanted to be an actress. Him telling me I should be a writer instead. Noticing how we crossed our legs the same way and had a similar sense of humor. Moments that made me understand that I am a product of both BD and Ken, of nature and nurture.

BD and I had another thing in common: he first met his father when he was a teenager, too. Being born into absence was our shared DNA, and so was the trauma that came with it. BD wasn't a villain, after all. He was a victim of rejection, just like me. And as such, he did what he was taught to do.

There's a growing body of scientific literature to support that grief and trauma can be passed down from generation to generation. In epigenetics, researchers study how gene expression is modified based on behavior and environment. In terms of trauma, that means that people who've experienced war, famine, or other forms of extreme stress can pass down genetic modifications to their offspring. Dr. Rachel Yehuda, professor of psychiatry and director of Traumatic Stress Studies Division at Mount Sinai's Icahn School of Medicine, has been at the forefront of this research. She and her team conducted a study of 32 Jewish men and women who had endured or observed torture, been interned at concentration camps, or went into hiding during the war. They also examined the genes of their adult children, finding that both parents and offspring had lowered cortisol levels compared to Jewish families who resided outside of Europe during the war. This is significant, as cortisol is the stress hormone that helps to counter adrenaline and calm the system. Yehuda concludes, "The gene changes in the children could only be attributed to Holocaust exposure in the parents." Research like Yehuda's suggests that our ancestors' life experiences have the power to leave lasting imprints for generations.

It wouldn't surprise me if on some very old branches of my paternal family tree there were ancestors who had also experienced abandonment and neglect. Living in these conditions creates a whole bunch of behavioral issues: co-dependency; fear of being left; insecurity and low self-worth; difficulty saying no and trouble self-regulating, especially big feelings like—you guessed it—anger. As a result, it can be hard to form healthy relationships, because it's difficult to trust others and even yourself.

It's my fault. There must be something wrong with me. I'm bad. These are common beliefs buried in the shameful wounds of trauma. For me, abandonment played out in countless familiar ways. As an adult, I often chose romantic partners who were emotionally cut off, were unaffectionate, or had a difficult time seeing me. I constantly made negative assumptions about what others thought of me (mirroring what I thought of myself). When my discomfort felt too big to cope with, I swiftly cut people out of my life, amputation style. And like many of us, I also self-abandoned.

Not long after I was diagnosed with cancer in my early 30s, BD visited me. We'd stayed in touch over the years—a visit here, a dinner there—but we struggled to form a solid relationship. After a few pleasantries, I learned why he had come in the first place.

"You need to get your affairs in order. You also need to figure out who's going to pull the plug if it comes to that." I was stunned. We hadn't created the kind of relationship that allowed for deeply personal and difficult talks like this, one that took an incredible amount of trust and tenderness—not to mention sensitivity. Maybe in his own awkward way he was only trying to be helpful. But it still hurt. *"Pull the plug"? Who says that?*

After his attempt at fatherly advice, he got up to leave. This visit lasted all of an hour. "Right-oh," he said, nodding my way as he stood at the door. And with that, he was gone.

I sat there frozen, not knowing how to process what had just happened. BD and I had barely talked about the basics, like where he was for most of my life or why he'd refused to acknowledge me. When we did connect, he preferred light banter.

Throughout my 20s, the pain stacked up, and no matter how many drugs, cocktails, or boys I devoured, I couldn't numb the truth: I wasn't wanted. His disconnected tone about DNRs and end-of-life planning did nothing to dispel this feeling.

Even with the parent who did want me, I sometimes felt like I was a burden. Growing up, I watched my mom work herself to the bone to make ends meet. Despite her efforts to hide her stress and show me love, the weight of caring for me and her two aging parents wrung her out. I witnessed the worry that came from not knowing how she would have enough money to pay the heating bill or make sure we had enough food to eat.

Maybe if I'd never been born, she'd be better off was a thought that played on a loop in my childhood . . . that is, until Ken showed up, making our family—and me—feel whole.

NO MUD, NO LOTUS

I was 38 when BD died. Our shared histories of grief and trauma were too big to heal in this lifetime, at least with each other. Neither of us had the emotional skills needed to tend to the wounds and regret between us, and that's OK.

It's safe to say that all of us have experienced trauma in our lives, in some capacity, whether it be financial insecurity, chronic illness, abuse, or injustice. And, like grief, trauma is something that few of us know how to care for. Some of us may not even recognize the ways trauma lives inside us. Though our world is becoming more trauma literate, for many of us it remains yet another taboo subject that we lock away (consciously or unconsciously).

Before writing this book, I was pretty clueless, too. I used to think of trauma as an "event," but, according to Gabor Maté, physician and trauma expert:

> Trauma is not what happened to you, it's what happened *inside* you as a result of what happened to you. And that's the good news. Because if trauma was what happened to you, there's nothing you can do to change that. But if the trauma is the wound that occurred inwardly, you can heal that wound at any time. So recognizing that trauma is an internal psychological wound with manifestations in your body actually allows you to heal it.

Maté's definition of trauma explains why two siblings may go through the same traumatic event (like their parents' acrimonious divorce) and have completely different responses to it. Or how two people can be in the same car accident and have completely different recoveries from similar injuries.

While there's no right or wrong way to react to trauma, there is a universal place to begin the healing process: your body. That's because trauma hides in our bodies, where it often remains dormant until something like a smell or a sound triggers it.

As we've explored, when our brains perceive a threat, our bodies instantly go into self-protection mode. This physiological response is designed to be temporary. But when trauma goes unaddressed, it often gets stuck in our bodies, continuing to signal that we're in danger even when we're not.

You're already familiar with the three main responses to perceived danger: fight (when we react with aggression), flight (when we react by leaving a situation), and freeze (when we react by going numb and possibly dissociating). Therapist and trauma expert Pete Walker popularized a fourth response, which he calls "fawn." This is when we react to threats by being overly people-pleasing or helpful as a way to defuse attacks. In his book *Complex PTSD: From Surviving to Thriving*, Walker writes: "Traumatized children often over-gravitate to one of these response patterns to survive, and as time passes these four modes become elaborated into entrenched defensive structures . . ."

Whatever our go-to response, the million-dollar questions is this: *How do we get unstuck?* Dr. Peter Levine, founder of Somatic Experiencing, a "body first" approach to healing, teaches that trauma requires us to learn how to discharge the stored energy from our trauma responses in order to restore our nervous systems and return to a sense of safety.

He was inspired to study stress on the animal nervous system when he realized that animals are constantly under threat of death yet show no symptoms of trauma. In order to return to homeostasis, animals in the wild release survival energy by shaking, trembling, yawning, breathing deeply, moaning, and so forth. This allows them to turn off the threat response by completely cycling through the experience. Whether we realize it or not, humans have this capacity, too. We can learn to actively engage in behaviors that support trauma and stress release. For example, shaking your whole body as a yogic practice has been around for centuries. Studies have shown that chanting "om" stimulates the vagus nerve, which sends the signal that a threat is no longer active. We'll dive into other methods in the "Caring for . . ." section below, but the point is, you can learn to silence the alarm bells and calm your system.

And here's why this is important: our nervous systems don't forget. If our threat response is left perpetually firing, it creates both physical and psychological problems, including severe dysregulation and even dissociation.

When Dad was dying, it *felt* like he was abandoning me. Even though I knew that wasn't true, my body didn't. So it's no surprise that it kicked up my own PTSD from the lack of relationship I had with BD, as well as my cancer diagnosis. No wonder my body felt like it was falling apart. Try as I might, my go-to tools to keep my shit together were failing. At some point, even my wellness practices started to feel like I was just leaning on hollow platitudes to cover up the depths of fear and pain I felt. That's when I knew I needed additional support to help me access the deeper, more hidden parts that needed tending.

CARING FOR GRIEF & TRAUMA

If this conversation is the medicine you need right now, set the intention that whatever comes up is OK. You don't need all the answers—you just need the willingness to explore.

Start with talk therapy: Both grief and trauma need to be witnessed, and one of the most healing things we can do for ourselves and others is to tell our stories. Tell your story.

Allow your feelings to move through your body: When you're ready, explore working with body sensations to reach the unexamined parts of yourself, possibly for the very first time. Deep breaths, full-body sobs, gut-wrenching screams, ecstatic dance—whatever helps you release your emotions. Here are some therapeutic tools that may help:

- **Somatic Experiencing (SE)** is a body-based approach to healing trauma and stress-related disorders, developed by Dr. Peter Levine. During a Somatic Experiencing session, the therapist will guide you through various physical sensations and experiences, such as breathing exercises, movements, and other techniques that help you become more attuned to your bodily experience. The therapist will also help you identify and release tension and stress from your body, using techniques such as gentle touch or guided imagery. Somatic Experiencing is a gentle, noninvasive therapy that can be helpful for a wide range of issues related to trauma and stress, including PTSD, anxiety, depression, and chronic pain. It can be particularly helpful for people who have difficulty expressing themselves in traditional talk therapy sessions.

- **EMDR (Eye Movement Desensitization and Reprocessing)** is a type of psychotherapy originally developed to treat symptoms associated with trauma and post-traumatic stress disorder (PTSD). During an EMDR session, the therapist will ask you to recall a traumatic memory while simultaneously tracking a visual or auditory stimulus, such as the therapist's finger moving back and forth or a series of beeps. This is thought to facilitate the processing of the memory and reduce the intensity of the associated emotions and physical sensations. EMDR is a relatively brief therapy, typically lasting between 6 and 12 sessions.

- **EFT (Emotional Freedom Techniques)**, also known as "tapping," combines elements of traditional Chinese medicine with modern psychology. It's based on the idea that negative emotions and beliefs can lead to imbalances in your body's energy system, which in turn leads to physical and emotional symptoms. Tapping on specific acupuncture points, while addressing the root cause of distress, sends a calming signal to the brain. This allows you to feel relaxed and in control. It's a simple and noninvasive technique that can be learned and practiced on your own. And it can be used to address a wide range of emotional and physical issues, including anxiety, depression, trauma, chronic pain, and addictions.

Trust your instincts: When it comes to finding the right healing modality, trust your instincts. Your healing may need you to experiment with different techniques in order to find what clicks for you. Remember, nobody does healing better than any other. We're all walking different roads to the same destination.

Trust that growth is possible: Most of us are familiar with the post-traumatic stress part, yet few of us have ever heard that growth is possible, too.

When we go through difficult or traumatic events, we often think of the negative impact they have on our lives. But did you know that some people can actually experience positive changes as a result of these experiences? This is known as post-traumatic growth (PTG). Developed by psychologists Richard Tedeschi, Ph.D., and Lawrence Calhoun, Ph.D., in the mid-1990s, the PTG theory suggests that people who've endured psychological struggle following adversity can often see positive growth afterward.

"People develop new understandings of themselves, the world they live in, how to relate to other people, the kind of future they might have and a better understanding of how to live life," says Tedeschi.

It's not about going back to your old self, but rather using the experience to become a better version of yourself. This can include things like having better relationships and feeling like you have a greater sense of purpose.

Everyone copes with trauma differently, so the process of PTG is different for each person. Some people may experience positive changes right away, while for others it may take longer. It's also important to understand that not everyone who experiences trauma will experience PTG, and that's OK. No one is expecting us to find silver linings. Personally, I found hope in even the mere existence of post-traumatic growth.

Trust that you are capable of doing this work: The Swiss psychologist Carl Jung believed that we keep circling around the same themes our entire lives, and with each passing orbit, we reach the next circle of meaning. From where I stand now, I believe that our orbiting is the mechanism of our healing. The waves of grief still pass over us, and the pain is still very real—sometimes as powerful as if it arrived on this morning's red-eye—but each time those waves come, we have a chance to tend to and nurture ourselves like we would a good friend. Think about it: We treat our friends and family with TLC because we love them. And when *we* are the ones hurting over unbearable losses or traumas, we are given the chance to love ourselves—truly, madly, deeply.

Processing trauma will likely feel intense, and that's normal. Trust that your spirit is able to breathe in the power of the entire universe. It can handle the matters of your heart as well.

And as the waves of emotion arise, you bravely allow them in and through. In and through. In and through, until the tides recede. And they will. You won't lose yourself, or if you do (temporarily), it's because you needed to process what wasn't working in order to heal.

Now, this doesn't mean that you'll be over the situation—the loss of your job, your health, or a loved one. Or that you condone any abuse or betrayal. It just means that you're willing to be restored so that you can carry on "with your one wild and precious life," as the poet Mary Oliver would say.

CHAPTER 6

Acceptance

The boundary to what we can accept
is the boundary of our freedom.

— TARA BRACH

If the word *acceptance* makes you feel uncomfortable or defeated, you're not alone.

Years ago, I remember hanging out backstage before delivering a keynote at a wellness conference when another speaker leaned over and asked me what the subject of my talk was. "The healing power of acceptance," I cheerfully shared. She paused.

"Oh. So you teach people how to give up?" she asked, with a furrowed brow.

Ugh. There was a reason I'd chosen this topic, hoping to untangle common misconceptions about acceptance with my audience (and now here with you).

Before we dive into acceptance and how it can help us in difficult times, let's clear up a few things.

Acceptance isn't giving up, settling, or denying the situation. Acceptance isn't being hunky-dory about what happened, either. As it relates to grief and loss, acceptance is about recognizing that life has changed, and we can no longer go back to what was. While we don't have to like it, here we are in a newly emerging reality. Acceptance helps us find a way forward that honors our unique journey and well-being.

Acceptance isn't passive; it's defiant. It's a way to rebel against shutting down, living in a destructive fantasyland, or losing hope. In a world that encourages quick fixes and black-and-white thinking, acceptance teaches us the expansive and revolutionary power of embracing the gray and *all* that comes with it.

If you can do that, you can do *anything*, my friend.

Think about it. When we spend all our time fighting or avoiding what is, we waste a lot of valuable energy—energy that could be channeled in a more fulfilling and productive direction. By accepting something challenging, we become more willing to roll up our sleeves and work with what we've got, as opposed to just sitting and stewing over the way we think things *should* be.

Like it or not, life won't always be sunny. It's not supposed to be. Yuck, I know! In our society, especially in the United States, there's a relentless emphasis on the many ways to find happiness by chasing something "out there." Sell your house and move overseas, lose 20 pounds and become a YouTuber, get thee to an ashram so you can find your bliss, hustle to conquer another brag-worthy achievement, and so on. And yet research shows that we're actually the most anxious country in the entire world.

Embedded in this collective "pursuit of happiness" is the notion that we can have whatever we want, whenever we want. In today's world, that often translates to something like *If I only put the right thoughts, efforts, and energy out there, I can attract whatever I desire and sidestep any of the bad stuff.* "Hey, universe, I'll take the rainbow, but hold the rain."

Unfortunately, these magical-thinking fantasies can sometimes do more harm than good. Especially when life falls apart in one fell swoop. You didn't choose *that*. You didn't fail. You didn't get sick, lose your spouse, or wind up in any other number of shit pickles because you put the wrong "vibes" out there. If that were the case, I'd be writing this from a women's correctional facility!

Speaking of harmful societal ideas, there's also a belief that we should just run out and replace what's lost in order to be whole again, as if it were a missing Tupperware lid. While well-intentioned (no one wants to see us in pain), these practices often make grieving and healing harder to achieve—for ourselves and for our loved ones. Someone or something unique and special to us can never be substituted.

Instead, a full range of pain and challenges will occur in life, no matter how healthy, conscious, resourceful, or spiritual we happen to be. In that way, acceptance grounds us and prepares us for the good times *and* the storms. It teaches us the bone-deep wisdom found in the Serenity Prayer:

"Grant me the serenity to accept the things I cannot change, the courage to change the things I can, and the wisdom to know the difference."

The opposite of acceptance is resistance. Fighting against the truth: *Maybe he'll come back.* Fighting with our egos: *I'm not the kind of person who falls apart.* Fighting against what we know we need to do, say, or feel: *Maintain a stiff upper lip.* And fighting with each other, instead of coming together: *It's all their fault.*

While I can't change what happened (I got sick, my dad got sick and eventually passed, life changed in ways I didn't want it to, and old traumas emerged as a result of these ruptures), I can change what I do *now*—how I proceed moving forward, how I grow and make the most of the precious, never-guaranteed time I have with my loved ones, with my dreams, and most importantly, with myself.

For many of us, resistance is our go-to mode. We'd rather deny, avoid, or brawl than face the truth of how our lives are changing or even what we've been through. But as the saying goes, "What we resist persists," keeping us stuck in pain and frozen in time.

Learning to *live* with cancer was my first big experience with acceptance. Learning to *live* with loss was my second. Like it or not, I couldn't change either situation. But I could use both of these experiences as catalysts for a more connected way of living.

If you are wrestling with fire-breathing dragons like this in your own life, this next story might help you expand your perspective.

HEALING VS. CURING

At many cancer hospitals, there's a beautiful closing ceremony and rite of passage for patients who make it to the other side of sick. The staff gather on the patient's last day of treatment to applaud them and ring a congratulatory bell, celebrating a clean bill of health, while honoring the team effort it took to get there. At long last, the patient is able to check the coveted "survivor" box—even if just temporarily.

But there are no boxes to check for people who live outside of them, and boy does this mess with our culture, which is far more comfortable with clear-cut (and often traditional) definitions. Man or woman. Married or single. Black or white. Fat or skinny. Healthy or sick, and on and on. You can't even get a frickin' bikini wax without offering up your health status. *Focus on my bush, please; my tumors are none of your business.*

In the beginning, I was caught up in the conventional medical paradigm, where you're either a patient in treatment or a survivor (aka "winner"; only losers lose their battle, after all—or so the unhelpful metaphors would have us believe). Naturally, I wanted to be a winner.

What would it take for that bell to ring for me? I wondered.

I've since discovered that true healing doesn't come from a finish line, bell, or box. It also doesn't come from a relentless drive to fix yourself—as if you're broken unless your life looks perfect.

For so many years, I tried everything I could to be in remission. When conventional medicine didn't have any options for me, I thought, *Screw this, I'll do it myself (just like everything else).*

I changed my diet and lifestyle. I fasted, cleansed, and detoxed. I left my toxic job. I spent long stretches at a Zen monastery to learn to calm the fuck down. I moved out of the city to the country, where the air was fresher and life was healthier. And I did a ton of soul-searching. All these changes were good in so many ways, improving my health, my well-being, and my overall quality of life.

There was just one glaring issue: my actions to heal were motivated by fear.

At my most extreme, I even elected to have a port—a small plastic medical device—surgically tunneled under my skin and attached to the large vein just above my heart. The port allowed me to experiment with very high doses of vitamin C (ascorbic acid—a vein burner), as well as IV hydrogen peroxide and ozone treatments. Several of these protocols are used for different reasons as part of integrative therapies, and now even Western medicine has started studying vitamin C as a supplement to more traditional therapies, like chemo.

PSA: While these kinds of alternative treatments can be helpful, I don't advocate forgoing conventional medicine—especially without highly *qualified* supervision. Just sayin'.

Did my holistic treatments help? Maybe, maybe not. One of my scans looked markedly better. But because my scans were often good, it was impossible to determine how or why. Was it the nature of my slow-growing disease or the nature of my choices or both? Why does one person with my rare cancer do well, while another doesn't? Here we go again with the "whys" . . .

Maybe if I'd kept grinding away in fear-based reactions, I would have reached my cancer-free goal. Or maybe I'd just be broke. None of these treatments were covered by my already too-expensive insurance. But since no one could tell me how long it would take to reach the finish line, or how effective these treatments would be, there was no end in sight.

Did I mention that my oncologist had no idea what I was doing? Afraid he would try to stop me, I kept quiet about my extracurriculars. I'll never forget the look on his face when he asked me if there was anything new going on. "Well, there is one thing," I said, lowering the neck of my shirt to reveal my port.

"What the heck is that?!" he said.

"I tried to cure myself—again," I replied, sheepish.

He agreed to surgically remove the device if I promised not to wander off the beaten path again without consulting him first. Fair enough. But the experience (and his alarmed expression) really got me thinking. I was spending 90 percent of my time running around trying questionable therapies that my highly qualified doc didn't sanction. What if I lived a long life *with* cancer, but missed out on the simple moments and everyday magic by wasting my days in worry?

I couldn't stomach that kind of regret, so I did what I rarely do. I quit. I quit trying to have perfect health. I quit comparing myself to other patients and coming up short. I quit blaming myself for getting sick *and* for not getting well. Most importantly, I quit seeing myself as anything other than whole.

And while I quit trying to cure myself, I never quit betting on myself.

This is how I learned that there was a difference between healing and curing. Curing takes place at the physical level. It's absolutely possible but never guaranteed. Healing, on the other hand, takes place at the spiritual level and is available to all of us—no matter who we are, what we look like, or where we come from. And just like love, healing never ends. In fact, we can be healing and dying at the very same time.

The only thing required to enter the healing path is the decision to do so. Nothing and no one can take it away from you—not even your own mortality. While figuring out how to truly accept this paradigm is by no means easy, know that on the other side of this awareness is a greater ease and appreciation for life, as well as a deeper compassion for yourself and others.

Accepting my disease freed me up to love my life, again. It allowed me to embrace living as a cancer "thriver"— someone who lives fully with cancer—who coexists with something that isn't easy or desired but doesn't define me, either. Identifying as a thriver helped me stop taking care of myself for *cancer* (or because "I have to") and start doing it for *me*. Because I deserve to feel good—and so do you. Now, instead of eating my vegetables or moving my body for cancer, I do healthy things so that I can have more energy and joy for my life. This may seem like a small mental shift, but for me it was epic.

Now, I'm not going to lie, some days are more triumphant than others. Healing is never linear. We zig and zag, take two steps forward and one step back. And that's OK. It's yet another thing I'm working on accepting.

Before Dad got sick, I thought I had a Ph.D. in acceptance, but after his terminal prognosis, the prospect of losing him demanded that I do some postgrad work. No matter how irrational and misplaced my feelings were, the little girl inside me was still terrified of being left. For a while, denial or gin or researching more medical procedures (that didn't exist) provided an excellent distraction from those feelings.

When I finally had to wake up and accept that the only thing left to do was to make Dad feel as comfortable and loved as possible, I didn't think I could do it. I wanted to keep running. But in actuality, my resistance was keeping me running in the opposite direction of love.

ACCEPTING LOSS

The hardest thing for any of us to accept is loss, especially when it comes to the death of someone we love or even our own mortality. As we've explored, *allowing* the pain of our losses is how we ultimately start feeling alive again. We may never "get over it." But over time, we become more adept at breathing again and moving forward.

As grief expert David Kessler writes:

> We must try to live now in a world where our loved one is missing. In resisting this new norm, at first many people want to maintain life as it was before a loved one died. In time, through bits and pieces of acceptance, however, we see that we cannot maintain the past intact. It has been forever changed and we must readjust. We must learn to reorganize roles, re-assign them to others or take them on ourselves.

This is not an easy process, but I agree wholeheartedly with Kessler. Accepting whatever reality we're in—no more summer boat rides together, no more inside jokes, no more random dance parties—is necessary to being fully present.

If you find that you're still not ready to accept what's going on in your life right now, no judgment here. As valuable as acceptance is, there are going to be times when you're just not there. And that's OK, too. If this is the case, I love the following insight from trauma expert Dr. Gabor Maté: "Acceptance also means accepting how downright difficult it can be to accept." Accept that it's really hard to accept and then stay open to accepting *someday*. And that's enough for now.

As his health hung in the balance, Dad was instrumental in teaching me even more about the power of acceptance. He gave me a trail of bread crumbs to follow as I watched him become softer and more self-accepting—finally allowing himself to believe that he was good enough and had done a good enough job at parenting, working, friendship, marriage, and life. He stopped being so embarrassed by his bald head and, in particular, about his overall appearance. Did he accept that he was going to die? I think so, because at a certain point, even the smallest things became worthy of celebration.

In Chapter 1, I talked about surrender and acceptance interchangeably, which, in a lot of ways, I think they are. Surrender and acceptance are the twin flames of leaning into our lives as they are. The main distinction, as I see it, is that acceptance happens in the head space, while surrender happens in the heart space.

We focus our energy on what we can do, versus things we have no control over. And then we give it over to love, to grace, to the mystery.

CARING FOR ACCEPTANCE

Now you might be thinking, *This is all well and good, but how do you actually put this advice into practice?* Breathing helps. Meditating helps. Reading everything by Buddhist teacher Tara Brach, author of *Radical Acceptance*, helps. And all the tips mentioned throughout this chapter certainly help. But here's what's helped me more than anything else:

Let go of the "shoulda, woulda, couldas": You know the nasty little suckers I'm talking about. The unproductive thoughts that keep us stuck in the past, beating ourselves up, or blaming others.

The "shoulda, woulda, couldas" mess up our ability to recognize all the goodness that's actually happening in our lives right now—even if the present moment also holds pain.

I should have taken better care of myself. I could have caught this sooner. I would have done things differently if I only knew. I could have called my dad more if I wasn't so selfish. I could have pushed harder for him to do XYZ. I should have allowed him to have that goodbye Zoom party with his friends (a suggestion he made that melted my brain and made me shout, "I'm not ready for that!").

To some degree, the "shoulda, woulda, couldas" are normal, especially when we remember how we humans evolved in order to stay safe. Who hasn't been a Monday-morning quarterback analyzing better outcomes in retrospect? We all do it. But when left unchecked, the Monday-morning quarterbacking makes it way harder to pick up the pieces and move forward. Which makes sense, as that retrospective focus is keeping us rooted in an unchangeable past. Yeah, I should have done all of those things, but the facts are clear: I didn't, and there's nothing I can do about it now.

Acceptance reminds us to be compassionate with ourselves. Some days, I'm on board with the limitations of my life; other days, not so much. Acceptance allows me to handle the highs, lows, and contradictions. To forgive life so I can spend more time healing.

Even if you've lost something or someone so important that it feels impossible to ever be happy again, love is still waiting for you. In fact, love never dies.

Tapping into that love is how we keep living fully. Loving ourselves through the pain. Through the difficult times and uncertainty. No matter what happens, choosing to love. People come, jobs go, money tightens, hearts get broken—love remains. This is how we survive and eventually thrive again.

Life is a terminal condition. We're all going to die, but how many of us will truly live? When you answer this question honestly, you will be changed in the best possible way, just like I have been.

Acceptance is what will help you get there.

CHAPTER 7

REST IN LOVE

The irony of man's condition is that the deepest need is
to be free of the anxiety of death and annihilation; but
it is life itself which awakens it, and so we must shrink
from being fully alive.

— ERNEST BECKER, *THE DENIAL OF DEATH*

For most of us, death remains our number one fear.

Yet end-of-life conversations are often taboo, which is
ironic considering it's the *one* thing every living being has
in common. We'll talk about other tough stuff like money,
fear, and the chlamydia we got from that rugby player
we met in a New York City bar in the '90s (or is that just
me?), before we'll go near that which will remain unspeak-
able. Instead, we shove death under the rug with other
unsightly things, like pennies and lint-covered Tic Tacs.

Our fear of death starts at a young age. My friend
Suzanne O'Brien, RN, founder of Doulagivers, an organization that offers end-of-life care training, says that our

first experiences with death often shape our fears around it. (Anyone else completely traumatized as a kid by *Bambi*?)

Many of us were raised by parents who thought it was best to shield us from the topic as a means of protection. But when we're shielded from conversations or even the acknowledgment of death, we wind up filling in the gaps with our own imagination, which is rarely accurate or helpful—especially when we're children. One reason adults might be hush-hush about death and mortality is that they have their own disordered relationship to it, so we pick up their baggage, too. So often, it's not that kids can't handle the truth but that their caregivers are ill-equipped to communicate openly about it.

One of my first experiences with death was that of my grandpa passing when I was nine years old. I was lucky to have a mom who sat me down and opted to brass-tacks his departure to me. She lovingly stated the facts. And for reasons I can't fully explain, I understood that he was gone, but that didn't mean my feelings for him were gone. To me, he was still Pops. I still loved him, and he was still with me. No one needed to explain that to me; it's just something I innately felt.

At his wake, I was so convinced of his continued presence that it was business as usual. I did what I always did when I said goodbye to him after a visit. I leaned over the casket to give him a kiss. Before I knew what hit me, my horrified neighbor swatted my ass. "That's disrespectful!" Thankfully, I had enough maturity (even though I had yet to reach double digits!) to know that this was her issue, not mine. FYI, grief expert Julia Samuel shares many wonderful approaches to talk to children about death in honest and age-appropriate ways. Her book *Grief Works* is for all ages and among the *most* helpful I've read. Can someone please drop one off at my old neighbor's house?

Honoring death as the natural and sacred passage it is goes against the grain of most everything we've been taught by our age-phobic culture—especially as women. We spend billions of dollars to prolong our lives and look as young as possible forever. Girls as young as 13 line up for Botox as a "preventive" measure against natural aging.

The message: your worth goes down as your age goes up.

Aging is a visual reminder of where we're *all* going—which scares the pants off us. Our fear of death is why many find comfort in religion and are endlessly fascinated by the cosmos. We desperately need to know the unknowable (or feel like we do) in order to feel a modicum of security in the vast uncertainty of our magnificent universe. So, we slather on the antiaging eye creams and focus our telescopes to the night sky, but when it comes to the inevitability of our mortality, we stubbornly stick our heads in the sand.

Then guess what happens? Someone close to us enters the final season of their lives, and we have no idea what to do, how to support them, or even how to be in our own skin. At some point, that person will be us. None of us has that much time left, so we might as well drag death out of the sterile and lonely shadows in order to start feeling more capable, connected, and empowered in our mortality.

TALKING ABOUT TALKING ABOUT IT

While no one teaches us what to say, as his days counted down, Dad was one person who did want to talk about death. It felt selfish for me to keep resisting, just because I was clueless and scared and extremely underprepared.

So, I googled it.

How do you talk about dying with someone who's dying? What do I say and not say? How do I do it without totally falling apart? I don't know how to do this—help!

Google suggested I start with small talk as a way to get the conversation going.

- Ask about his first job: "Shoveling snow in the neighborhood. Then my brother Jay signed up for a paper route. I was 10, he was 13. Jay quit, and my dad made me take over because you can't leave a guy in the lurch without his paper."

- Ask if he ever played a crazy practical joke: "I'm not a prankster with someone else's feelings."

- Ask what his first car was: "A 1958 Ford Thunderbird. That was my baby! I was working construction at West Point and had a pretty good paycheck sealing parking lots. I loved tooling around in that car. I was the hottest guy in the neighborhood."

After some practice, I got brave and asked a question of my own.

"Do you want a foot rub with some cream?"

"No, but I want a Cheeto," he replied.

Carole, my therapist, told me to take it a step further with a technique she called "talking about talking about it," meaning start a conversation about *how* to approach the topic and what might happen when you do. "Let him know that you will likely have big emotions around it," she said. I had a vision of sitting down with a supersize tissue box and a Valium patch as she continued, "As long as that's OK, and not too painful or stressful for him, tell him that you're willing to try." Sounded reasonable to me.

Here's a good place to mention that if you feel compelled to broach this kind of conversation, your loved one may not be open to it, and that's OK. Not everyone nearing death wants to address these topics head-on. Just as there is a lot of diversity in how we, as individuals, want to live, there's diversity in how we want to die, too.

I recently learned a story about an actress named Suzanne Smith, who died at age 45 after living with breast cancer for 20 years. Suzanne was adamantly opposed to having these conversations with her loved ones. Weeks before she died, if someone brought up the word *hospice*, God help them. True to her spirit, in her death and in her life, she was a spitfire.

Even after Suzanne was in hospice and had what is known as "the death rattle," a sign that death is imminent, she managed to eke out, "I . . . want . . . to . . . live." And she did, for two more days. That may not sound like a lot, but given her condition, the nurses assured her family that it was nothing short of remarkable.

When someone is dying, we have to respect and even celebrate not only their desires but who they are. One way or another, they will let you know what they need.

With Carole's expert help, the next time I saw my dad, I sat down with a wad of tissues bundled in my pocket and said, "I'd like to talk to you about how to talk about death, Dad. I want to do this as best as I can, but I'm probably going to be awkward, fearful, and, at times, tearful. Is this something you'd still like to do?"

"I'd like that very much, love. I don't have many people I can talk to about this, and it's on my mind a lot these days. To be honest, it can be quite lonely."

I started by asking him if there was anything he wanted to experience before he died.

"I want to have a little fun every day." A game of gin rummy would suffice, he said.

After a pause, I ventured further. "Are you scared, Dad?"

"Not really. I'm just sad to leave. I want to know how all your stories are going to unfold." Who his brother's grandkids would marry. Where Brian and I would move. What Mom would plant in the garden that spring.

It's easy to shut down conversations like this because we're afraid to get them wrong or to be seen as a downer or negative. "Let's talk about something *nice*. You're going to be fine," we say. But maybe they'll never be fine again, and not talking about that possibility isn't fine, either. Addressing the elephant in the room gave Dad palpable relief. Talking about what was on his mind allowed him to feel less alone. It cleared space for us to find joy in the simple everyday moments that remained.

Knowing Dad felt less alone made *me* feel less alone, too, not to mention more present with him, which is what I'd wanted all along. And oh, the gin rummy we played.

TAKING THEIR LEAD

A few weeks after our talk, Dad began sleeping more. Detaching from his surroundings and relationships. "I can feel him withdrawing, fading away," Mom painfully confessed. Like an animal who instinctually isolates when they're vulnerable.

But according to hospice, social withdrawal is another natural part of the dying process. It's the person's way of starting to let go of their physical life, and as hard as it is for those who remain, that physical life includes their loved ones. When this happens, family members can feel hurt or maybe worried that they've upset the person who is dying. Or they can take it personally, not understanding why their loved one is showing less interest in connection.

In reality, this distance is very understandable. Dad often joked, "Dying takes a lot out of you." From observing him, I second that. The body slowly breaks down. It can take 45 minutes to swallow a pill. Getting to and from the bathroom looks as tricky as walking a high wire. And don't even get me started on bathing. Dying is fucking exhausting.

Because extended family members and friends weren't around day-to-day, they had a hard time grasping what little energy he had. I imagine that in their minds, Ken was still Ken. And though his spirit was as strong as ever, his body and presence weren't. Sometimes they wanted him to do what *they* wanted to do or talk about what *they* wanted to talk about. If he wasn't open to exploring certain topics (often because he didn't have the energy or desire to do so), they might get offended, perhaps not realizing that they were centering their needs over his.

Having unrealistic (or even any) expectations of the dying is a surefire way to drive a wedge between you, the person you're losing, and everyone else. Expectations can also be a way to mask our torn-up feelings about the enormity of the loss we're facing. While we need to care for our emotions, we may also need to lower our standards, do our best to go with the flow, and once again remind ourselves that everyone is doing the best they can during a really shitty and difficult time.

When someone is dying, a piece of *everyone* is dying with them. None of us are prepared for this. Even if someone has a lot of experience with loss, unwieldy emotions will still come up because we're all flailing around in anticipatory grief and existential mourning.

LISTEN WITH YOUR FULL BEING

Listen to the person who is dying with your ears *and* your heart. Pick up what's being said and not said. Difficult stuff to do, I know. We'll get it wrong a lot, we'll mess up when we're trying to step up, but our willingness to try is the most generous way we can show our love when people need it most.

Or as Dr. Maya Angelou put it, "People will forget what you said, people will forget what you did, but people will never forget how you made them feel."

The same is true for our pace. Oftentimes we move really fast around the dying—not just physically but verbally. Maybe that's because we're jacked up on adrenaline, so focused on trying to get it right or to avoid discomfort that we fail to slow down and simply be. But when we don't know how to slow down, the person we're most concerned about may actually wind up feeling invisible. We're still hyperconnected, after all, keeping up with the pace of our busy lives and busy worlds. But the person who is dying is winding down and getting more introspective. We're in two very different places, so it takes awareness to recalibrate our energy.

If we're unaware of things like our anxiety, we might talk over the person or even avoid eye contact. I noticed this happening to my dad. I'd watch as uncomfortable people made *him* feel uncomfortable, and he'd eventually give up on trying to be included by them. This smashed my heart (and poked my protective instincts).

When people didn't make space for him to participate in conversation, even unintentionally, I was sure to make it *for* them. "Excuse me . . . what were *you* saying, Dad?" Or sometimes I'd just take the direct approach: "You're interrupting him. . . . Go ahead, Dad."

Whether my conversation crossing-guard approach was helpful or not, the point here is that social dynamics change up until the very end and beyond. The more connected and committed we are to paying attention to our behavior, the healthier it is for everyone.

KEEP LIVING

A few weeks before Dad slipped into a coma-like state, unable to communicate, he asked me to go to CVS and buy him Bioré strips. "You know, those strips that get the blackheads off your nose? Pick up some of those and let's do facials." Dying or not, Dad was all about looking "spiffy," after all.

When I was growing up, he spent more time in the bathroom than I did! He'd blow-dry his hair and set it perfectly with Vitalis for Men hair spray. I was more of an Aqua Net gal myself, and I definitely did not have the self-taught salon-quality skill he had somehow acquired.

Dad was so good with hair that my mom and I nicknamed him "Kenzo," and eventually trusted him with our own locks. When we needed a color touch-up, he'd head to CVS to get the classiest color he could find. For me, it was "Sahara" blonde.

One of the last things Dad did before he died was touch-up Mom's hair. He didn't want to leave without spiffing her up one last time. He needed everything to be in order—including her roots. His way of giving us everything he possibly could.

But with so little time left, I couldn't understand why he cared about blackheads. The more I thought about it, the more I realized what Dad was teaching me. I didn't want to eat, shower, or see anyone. Self-care had officially left the building. During my lowest, most depressing moments, I'd find myself thinking, *What's the point? If we're all going to die, what difference does all this self-care make? I clearly need to find a new profession.*

Enter the Bioré strips. Within a few weeks, Dad would be cremated. Yet here he was, caring for his pores and himself. Not because he wanted to look good for anyone else but because he wanted to look and feel good for himself.

It made me think of those Tibetan sand mandalas. A team of Buddhist monks tirelessly work building colorful geometric sand designs in intricate detail. The mandalas represent many things, including our journey from ignorance to enlightenment. Once the mandala is done, and the ceremonies and public viewings are over, the monks destroy the beautiful work of art by sweeping it away—signifying that nothing lasts forever.

In this way, our bodies are like mandalas, too. Beautiful. Intricate. Full of wisdom, and, despite their fragility, worthy of spiffing until our very last breath.

DR. PORN AND HOSPICE

Mom called and asked me if I could come over and give her a break. "I'd love to take a shower and actually find the time to blow-dry my hair. Can you take care of Dad?" It never ceased to amaze me how little it took for her to recharge and "feel like a new woman."

Once I got there, Dad and I picked up where we left off in our game of gin rummy. We usually only got a few turns in before he nodded off. Just then the doorbell rang, and there was the hospice doctor. This was the first time I had met him. I invited him in and steadied myself and my COVID mask for the conversation about Dad's status. The pandemic was good for one thing: those damn masks helped me hide my quivering lips whenever I was attempting to choke back tears. (Having become more emotionally brave, I'd retired the anchovies and dead mice by then.)

"We're going to take good care of you, Ken," the doctor said. "And we're going to make sure that you're comfortable, but at this point you know we can't fix the disease, right?"

"Yes, I do, Doctor," Dad replied, as I could feel the tears welling.

"Now is a good time to tie up any loose ends, too. Have you sorted out your will yet?"

"Yes, I'm all set there."

"Have you chosen if you want to be buried or cremated?"

"Yes. I've decided to be cremated."

"Are you religious?"

"I follow my own path with that."

"Well, if you want to see the chaplain, just let us know and we'll send him."

You got this, Kris. You got this. Hold fast. Damn, this was rough.

"What about porn?"

My sorrow instantly shut down. Dad looked stunned, so the doctor continued, "While you can still get around with your walker, you might want to get rid of it if you have any. This way no one else will have to deal with it after you're gone."

Dad burst into laughter. "That won't be a problem, Doctor." From then on, "Dr. Porn," as we took to calling him, was Dad's favorite, straight-shooting visitor.

At first, hospice scared me because I was a newbie and had no clue what to expect. For instance, I didn't know that hospice was a service, not a place (though there are hospice facilities). Multiple times per week, a team of compassionate nurses and other professionals skilled at end-of-life care came to check on Dad.

They monitored his vitals and adjusted his medications. They groomed and bathed him, allowing my mom more time to just be his wife. They ordered medical supplies and equipment like a hospital bed, wheelchair, and walker. They even offered grief counseling for us all and continued to provide it for over a year past his death. During the final hours, they were with us 24-7, teaching us what was happening and how to respond to it.

When we freaked out because Dad's stomach was filling up with fluid, they gently explained that this was normal. His liver was starting to shut down, which was why his legs were also so swollen. Luckily, they were able to drain his abdomen every other day, providing him relief.

The nurses taught us how to use the "comfort kit" they'd made for us—a white paper bag filled with morphine and other prescriptions to help with any breakthrough pain. Comfort kits are designed to keep patients out of the hospital—the last place Dad wanted to be.

According to the Hospice Foundation of America, many individuals and families could benefit from hospice care sooner than they get it, but people don't often know how to access the services. Some are afraid to discuss it or don't want to concede "defeat." Some wait for a physician to suggest it, unaware that they can initiate care on their own, as long as eligibility criteria are met.

A person doesn't have to be bedridden or in their final days of life to receive care, either. When there's a significant decline in health, and comfort is the only thing left to give, hospice is there. Here in the U.S., hospice is covered by Medicare, and in almost every state by

Medicaid. It's also covered by most private health insurance to varying degrees.

BE MINDFUL OF YOUR ENERGY

Another thing the hospice team taught us was to be mindful of our own energy when we were in his space. "Though he is now in the active phase of dying, just because he can't talk to you, doesn't mean he can't hear you or pick up the vibes. Talk to him. Tell him you love him. But *don't* bring stress here or talk about things you wouldn't talk about in front of him."

This made me realize just how sensitive we *all* are to energy—especially when our own energy is diminished. We absorb vibes like little sponges. We're impacted by feelings and moods (ours and other people's). That's why learning to care for and protect our energy is so valuable.

When friends and family got overly emotional, Dad's pain would increase. He'd be agitated and need more morphine when they left. I suspect it was because he took on their pain in addition to his own but was totally incapable of doing anything about it. Some folks understood when we'd asked them to be mindful of the energy they brought into the room; others didn't (they weren't allowed back).

Dad's coma-like state lasted five days. I sat with him and caught him up on "what was doin'," just as I would when he could respond. "The next-door neighbors painted their house white; it looks really nice." Or I'd just quietly work on a jigsaw puzzle, keeping him company. "Dad, I'm having a heck of a time finding this one piece," I'd say. "It's probably right in front of my eyes, but damn if I can see it." Turns out I'd never find it. The puzzle would never be complete again, and neither would our family.

At a certain point, those transitioning stop eating and drinking. I mean, I guess I knew that. I just assumed they'd be given intravenous food and fluids or *something*. But the only thing Dad's body had energy to process was the completion of life. We moistened his dry throat with a small wet sponge on a lollipop stick and softened his chapped lips with olive oil. Day turned into night as Dad hung on, holding fast to life.

The next morning, everything changed. His breath slowed to a raspy crawl. His moans grew fainter and fainter. His skin illuminated. My mom lit candles, and I played soft classical music. Together, we created a sanctuary for his passing. The dogs came in and out, curling up at the foot of the bed.

Mom sat on one side of him, and I sat on the other. She held his heart, and I held his hand. Her breath deepened on the inhale and "whooshed" on the exhale, as if she were leading a holy meditation. My breath automatically followed. With each rise and fall, I could feel Dad relax.

Instinctively, Mom knew to coach him with the sweetest encouragement.

"You're doing such a good job at this, my love. I am so *proud* of you."

"You can do this, my love. It's going to be OK."

"We love you so much. And we're going to really miss you. But you can go whenever you're ready. We're going to be OK. You're going to be OK, my love."

Watching her shepherd him through this passage with such powerful tenderness left me awestruck. It was as if the deepest, most sacred parts of her maternal and spiritual instincts were allowing her to open the doors to eternity for her precious love to walk through.

As Dad took his final breath, I heard what sounded like a timid little boy's voice. Though I have no idea what he was actually experiencing, this vulnerable, childlike sound reminded me of the first day of school, when you don't know anyone and hope to make new friends. Or that moment of excitement and pulsing nerves right before you jump off a cliff into a warm lake. These thoughts and images felt somewhat comforting. They made me feel like he wasn't leaving us; he was heading off to a new adventure.

We watched him as he moved into the unknown, still straddling both worlds, yet so much further out of reach. And right as we were about to lose him fully, the most beautiful smile spread across his face. I've never seen anything like it. He looked so happy, peaceful, and, most of all, relieved. It was as if he was being welcomed by people who loved him. No one had to tell him it would be OK anymore—it just was.

As our amazing nurse called his time of death, Mom and I just sat there in awe, tears streaming down our own smiling faces. "Dad, we're not happy you're gone, we're happy you're at peace."

Rest in love, Dad. Rest in love.

CARING FOR THE DYING

This was a tender chapter to write and likely one to read. If you're in the season of life where these stories and teachings apply to you, I hope my observations help illuminate your path. The bulk of my guidance and insights are woven into my stories, so you may want to review this chapter again. Here are a few other useful nuggets that helped me, too.

Get support *before* you think you need it: I shared this tip earlier, and I could probably include it in every chapter. Regardless of how incredibly capable you are, you are not invincible, and neither is your body. It's easy to underestimate the toll this experience takes on you, your health, and your mental well-being. Don't wait until you're a puddle on the floor; get ahead of this, and trust me when I say you'll need support, pal. It's really not negotiable. Surrender to it.

Breathe and check in with yourself: Once again, stay connected to your breath. Notice how you're breathing when you're with the person; notice if you're holding your breath. If you feel your heart racing, try slowing your breath down. Go to the bathroom if you need privacy to ground yourself. If you're like me, it's easy to dissociate or feel like you're having an out-of-body experience when you're flooded with emotions. I'll say it again: basically every weird thing going on is normal.

Emulate the energy you admire: Think about a person whose energy you love to be around, someone who makes you feel really good. You leave your time together feeling more buoyant than when you arrived. For me, people like that exude calmness and joy, they're easy to talk to, and they're wonderful listeners. This is the kind of energy we want to emulate when we're lucky enough to be with someone who is transitioning.

Oh, and one more thing. You're doing a really great job with this really tough stuff. If I could hug you right now, I would.

Let's keep going.

CHAPTER 8

Beyond the Stars

Now Besso has departed from this strange
world a little ahead of me. That means nothing.
People like us . . . know that the distinction
between past, present, and future is only
a stubbornly persistent illusion.

**— ALBERT EINSTEIN, ON THE PASSING
OF HIS FRIEND BESSO**

Before Dad died, I'd heard about some incredible deathbed experiences that suggest that the serenity of the afterlife is a real phenomenon. Like the story of a man who had a vivid dream of a relative visiting him. He awoke with a warm feeling in his heart, as if the visit had actually happened, only to find that his relative had died a few hours earlier.

Or the incredible experience of my colleague Anita Moorjani. In 2006, after a four-year battle with cancer, Anita fell into a coma and was given hours to live.

As my doctors gathered to revive me, I jour-
neyed into a near-death experience (NDE). The
feeling of complete, unconditional love was unlike
anything I'd known before. It was totally undis-
criminating, as if I didn't have to do anything to
deserve it, nor did I need to prove myself to earn it.
To my amazement, I became aware of the presence
of my father, who'd died ten years earlier. *Dad,
you're here. I can't believe it!* I wasn't speaking those
words, I was merely thinking them—in fact, it was
more like feeling the emotions behind the words,
as there was no other way of communicating in
that realm other than through emotions.

Anita goes on to describe how she was given a choice
in that realm. She could return to her physical form or
continue on in this new realm. "I chose the former, and
when I regained consciousness, my cancer began to heal.
To the amazement of my doctors, I was free of countless
tumors and cancer indicators within weeks. Since then,
I've heeded the call to share this powerful story—and
divine lesson—with the world: Love yourself fully. That's
what you're here to do."

Stories like these comforted me before Dad made his
transition. But after remembering the beaming expression
on his face when he died, I couldn't get enough of them,
even as a part of me wondered, *Could this be real?*

It's remarkable that people tend to describe near-death
experiences in a strikingly similar manner, which has led
some experts to believe in the existence of an afterlife.
Professors of psychiatry at the University of Virginia Jim
Tucker and Jennifer Kim Penberthy have delved into the
study of near-death experiences, after-death communi-
cations (where individuals claim to have been visited by

a deceased loved one), and children with memories of a previous life. Through their research, they have suggested that consciousness transcends our physical reality.

In his book *Return to Life*, Tucker described a young boy named Ryan Hammons, who could mysteriously recount specific details about a Hollywood agent in a previous life. Tucker was able to confirm that 55 of Hammons's claims matched the real-life experiences of Marty Martyn, a Hollywood agent who died in 1964.

Christopher Kerr, M.D., Ph.D., palliative care physician, end-of-life researcher, and author of *Death Is But a Dream*, teaches us that end-of-life experiences represent a continuity between and across lives. Through his research with dying patients, he discovered that in their final hours, many people experience peaceful visions.

Dr. Kerr tells the story of a patient named Mary: "One day, she starts cradling a baby that nobody can see." Mary's first child was stillborn. Mary had confided in her sister about the baby but no one else. Her grief was so powerful, she had to bury it. "Mary, like so many dying patients, had physical wounds that could not be cured, yet her spiritual wounds were tended to. Often these visions—vividly real to the person experiencing them—are of people who have died before them, and they provide a great sense of comfort, peace and even joy."

While it may be hard to understand what's happening in these moments, Dr. Kerr encourages us to not dismiss them just because we don't have enough data or tools to explain them. "There's this assumption that people have these visions because their brains are changing, becoming deoxygenated, or they are medicated and confused, but that's not the case. We know that by looking at the brain; it's not changing biologically or functionally. I think people are changing very much spiritually," he says.

When I considered Dr. Kerr's words, I was comforted. I may not be able to objectively prove that Dad had changed spiritually, but that was what I felt. And when I thought about it, I realized that I was changing spiritually, too.

SIGNS & SYNCHRONICITY

Two days after Dad died, my mom and I went for a walk on the beach. It was Valentine's Day, my 18-year cancer-versary, and her first Hallmark holiday without him. Dad would have called me and said, "Hey, love, how's my valentine today?" I miss those words so much. As our feet sank into the warm sand, I secretly searched for signs. Not dramatic thunderbolt kinds of signs . . . just affirming indications of Dad's continued love.

In grief, we often focus on what (or who) is no longer there in front of us. We naturally notice the *absence* of the person we love. A bed or chair they no longer occupy. Clothes that still hold their scent but hang empty day after day. Special moments like holidays or birthdays, where their nearness is so deeply missed.

My eyes can still find those places, years later, by simply observing the absence of Dad and, if I'm not careful, telling my heart he's just gone. But that's not what I want to believe. So I ask my eyes to see his *presence*, instead of just his *absence*.

After walking in silence for a while, Mom asked how I was feeling. "Bittersweet," I said. *I'm here. Dad's not.* He's not here to be thankful that I'm here. He's not here to see all the changes I will make in the coming years, many guided by his advice, and his voice, which I continually hear in my heart. He's not here to see me fall and get back up again. *And yet, maybe he is . . . guiding me in a new way,* I thought. In contemplating his continued presence, I found myself more open than I'd ever been to having faith in that which is unseen.

As we walked out farther, arriving at the place where nothing but our grief existed, I saw it. *"Oh my God, Mom. Look straight ahead!"* There in the distance were two long-stem red roses standing at attention in the sand. One for each of us. Instantly, I started to cry. Mom did, too. We hugged, then held hands as we marveled over these beautiful signs from above, staying there for what seemed like hours. *He's still here,* I thought. *He's still here.* Eventually, we made our way back to the parking lot, roses in hand.

As we were getting into the car, I happened to glance into the first-floor apartment next to where we were parked. There I saw a man in his living room, hunkering down in his La-Z-Boy to watch a show on his TV. The title credits read "Surviving Death."

I got so many chills I thought I should take a COVID test. *Hi, Dad. Thanks for letting me know what's doin'.*

But wait, this story gets wilder. As we drove home, I remembered something. That very morning, Brian had been struggling with whether or not to get my mom red roses, like he'd done for me.

"Is it weird to give them to her? What should I write on the card? Will it make her miss him even more? . . . I don't know what to do," he said.

"Babe, if you're so conflicted about it, then they're not yours to give. It's OK. Let's just spend time with her," I replied.

Recalling our conversation and looking at the roses, I smiled. As it turned out, Dad already had it covered.

Even when we have experiences like this and are filled with comfort, it's normal to have second thoughts. Personally, I'm a thinker. I like to analyze, and I love data. So my mind often drifted to wondering: *Were the roses in the sand just a coincidence?* Maybe, maybe not. What about the TV show? It's not like Dad could send me a notarized letter in the mail: *Yes, Kristin, that was me.*

Apparently, I'm not alone in noticing coincidences. Many people have observed coincidences in their lives. A study conducted by Dr. Bernard Beitman, a psychiatrist and founder of The Coincidence Project, in 2009, found that about one-third of the general population also notices coincidences. However, Dr. Beitman emphasizes that what truly matters is the personal significance that a coincidence holds for the individual experiencing it, whether in the moment or in hindsight. In other words, the subjective interpretation of a coincidence is more important than the mere fact that it occurred.

The synchronicities I experienced after Dad died were certainly not insignificant to me. Partly because they felt like winks from Dad. So I remained open to the idea and continued asking for signs—just to be sure. The more I asked for, the more I got.

A few days later, I desperately wanted to hear his voice again. I was walking around the mall, shopping for shit I didn't need to fill the hole I would never fill, when I began worrying that one day I'd forget what his voice sounded like. *I miss you so much, Dad . . .*

Just then my phone rang.

I looked at the number and it was Dad! *Wait, what's happening?! Is it really him?* I quickly picked up the call, filled with confusion and hope as my heart started pounding.

"Please leave a message and I'll return your call as soon as possible." It was his voice mail. I must have butt-dialed it by accident. But that felt unlikely. Even if he was on my "recent call" list, I've never butt-dialed anyone—I don't even have a butt! I'm a writer. It's a pancake. But sure enough, there was Dad's voice, coming through loud and clear at the exact moment I needed it.

As these experiences kept piling up, my brain naturally zoomed out to the bigger picture. What does this all mean? The "me" before Dad died had a more limited view of life, perhaps allergic to anything that smacked of religion or organized faith. Now, his loss was driving a deep curiosity about the nature of this universe.

In *The Grand Biocentric Design: How Life Creates Reality*, medical doctor and scientist Robert Lanza explores his theory of biocentrism—that living beings and consciousness create the universe and reality, not the other way around. So if consciousness can exist outside the universe—which contains all of space and time—consciousness is therefore timeless. He writes, "The biocentric view of the timeless, spaceless cosmos of consciousness allows for no true death in any real sense. When a body dies, it does so not in the random billiard-ball matrix but in the all-is-still-inescapably-life matrix."

To further explain his theory, Lanza likens consciousness to music played on an old phonograph:

> Listening to the music doesn't alter the record itself. Depending on where the needle is, you hear a certain song. This is the present—the music before and after the song is the past and the future. In like manner, every moment endures in nature always. The record doesn't go away. All "nows," like all songs on the record, exist simultaneously, although we can only experience it piece by piece. . . . Immortality doesn't mean a perpetual existence in time—it resides outside of time altogether.

Heady stuff, I know. But these ideas make me think that even if we can't pinpoint the exact location of our deceased loved ones on a GPS, they're still out there, playing their unique "music" in some form or fashion.

That's because energy cannot be created or destroyed; it can only be changed from one form to another. It's the first law of thermodynamics, y'all!

Energy never dies. The same is true for love. They're the alpha and omega, the beginning and end. No matter what happened, who we lost, or how lost we feel, we are all an essential part of that energy and always will be. Every time we tap into the power of love—connecting to the goodness of it, the joy inherent in it, the peace that emanates from it—we are connecting to the never-ending energy of the ones we've lost.

THE BIG QUESTIONS

Who am I? Why am I here? What am I supposed to be doing with my life? What happens when we die—do we just stop existing, or is there an afterlife? If we go somewhere, is Dad there? What about God and my cat Crystal?

Your big questions might look different than mine, just as your shit pickles may look different than mine. Nevertheless, our existential longing becomes more urgent when life falls apart or when death or grief come knocking. And yet, faith is something many of us struggle with, myself included. But as someone who's had serious doubts about trusting an invisible force, I've also had moments of clear knowing.

For example, after my grandpa passed, I remember trying to piece together what happens when we die. I imagined that death was like a hidden room inside our house. The people we lost were still close to us in that room, we just couldn't access them with our five senses. I didn't fear death, because I was confident that it wasn't final. I missed Grandpa. I missed my cat. But I knew that I'd see them again. And that one day, I'd be able to access that room.

Unbeknownst to me at the time, in the 1910 sermon delivered after King Edward VII died, an Oxford divinity scholar named Henry Scott Holland declared:

> Death is nothing at all. It does not count. I have only slipped away into the next room. Nothing has happened. Everything remains exactly as it was. I am I, and you are you, and the old life that we lived so fondly together is untouched, unchanged. Whatever we were to each other, that we are still. . . . There is absolute and unbroken continuity. What is this death but a negligible accident? Why should I be out of mind because I am out of sight? I am but waiting for you, for an interval, somewhere very near, just round the corner. All is well. Nothing is hurt; nothing is lost. One brief moment and all will be as it was before. How we shall laugh at the trouble of parting when we meet again!

It strikes me as a bit uncanny that I'd randomly come up with this idea, not aware that 62 years before my birth, when I was mere stardust, a random guy, across time and space, would float the same idea. Me in my bedroom surrounded by my stuffed animals, him addressing a congregation. Maybe there's something to this hidden room theory.

This felt like a sturdier explanation than what my grandma, who modeled a very eclectic kind of spirituality, might have taught me. One minute we were lighting candles and praying the rosary, the next we were writing down names of people who pissed us off and putting them in the freezer "to ice them out." In second grade, she told me about hexes, and I remember trying to practice using them on the mean girls at school. My spells must have backfired, because everyone got boobs before me.

One day, Grandma discovered that my mom had a tarot card deck. She immediately summoned me to hunt down the contraband and bring it to her—the devil cards must be cast out. Now mind you, this was a woman who smoked cigars and read the ashes to tell the future, but somehow tarot cards were a bridge too far. Questioning her faith or her superstitions was pointless. So, I army-crawled into Mom's bedroom, located the enemy in question next to some incense and other suspicious paraphernalia, like lavender oil, and brought the deck to Grandma. She wrapped the cards in a silk scarf and carefully disposed of them, as if they were a military-grade IED.

Grandma's talk of hexes, ashes, and the rosary did nothing to help me have a clearer relationship with faith. Each of her whims seemed detached from any cohesive idea about spirituality. It was all very confusing, but life with Grandma was never dull and kinda fun, too.

The year Grandpa died, Mom decided I needed some legit spiritual direction. "It's time for you to be baptized."

"Great! I want to pick my religion," I responded.

"Oh yeah? What do you want to be?"

"Jewish."

I had no idea what that meant. But based on my limited social life, I thought Jewish people threw great parties.

Overhearing this conversation from the living room, Grandma's voice boomed, "No, you are Catholic." Off I went to Father Elsinghorse.

On obligatory holidays, Grandma cornered me with a comb and marched me to church, a disastrously boring experience. I longed to be flying through the neighborhood on my Huffy bike instead of being stuffed into a satin dress and shiny shoes—my personal hell. Luckily, Grandma didn't like it much, either (despite her rosary habits), so the torture only occurred biannually.

When it came to end-of-life directives, Grandma's wishes were very clear. She wanted to be buried "like Tutankhamen," only Grandma's "tomb" would be her car, and it would contain her sewing machine. If the afterlife existed, she was assured to be independent and fashionable.

My grandfather's side of the family was a whole different bowl of holy water—pious believers, and devoted to public service. Ever guided by his evangelical Episcopalian faith, my great-great-grandfather Salmon P. Chase was the senator of Ohio, the chief justice of the Supreme Court, and secretary of the treasury in Lincoln's cabinet. He established our national banking system and slapped the slogan "In God We Trust" on our coins. While that phrase on money had a political purpose—implying that God was on the Union side of the Civil War—it was also meant to help save folks from becoming "heathens."

Grand Pop would have likely been horrified by my fluid, feral, and often fickle faith. Many decades later, I'm a deep seeker and a rigorous questioner. There's so much I am open to learning, yet I have some clarity around what I do and don't believe. For example, I don't believe in divine judgment, punishment, or biblical folklore. I do believe in a loving energy that connects us all. I don't believe that God is the sole provider of meaning or morals. Or that the divine is so delicate it can't be challenged or questioned. I subscribe to the power of prayer (asking) and meditation (listening), and I feel comforted when I talk to angels, guides, and the God of my understanding—regardless of whether or not anyone or anything exists or can hear me. Simply put, it feels good to connect, and that's enough for me.

My therapist thinks it's no surprise that I've struggled with faith, saying, "When you had a hard time trusting your original caretakers, it's difficult to trust the bigger caretaker."

Drop that mic, Carole.

That said, I'm finding that even the slightest willingness to trust in something greater helps me keep the door of faith open. Is my doubt gone? Hell no. But that's OK, too.

I share all this because not everyone has an easy time with religion or spirituality. It can be confusing, dogmatic, and just plain weird. And yet, folks who aren't sure or just don't buy it are often ridiculed or treated as if they're not "evolved" enough or trustworthy. Faith is a feeling, not a fact. It can't be forced. It's a personal choice and practice that's unique to each of us.

In today's world, faith can even be contentious. God is often trotted out like a puppet in our culture wars or is used as a weapon to separate and control us, especially women. The disingenuous and dangerous nature of these strategies not only diminishes how we think of God, but it turns many of us off to the very existence of a force beyond our knowing.

One thing is clear: Whatever the shit pickle du jour, people in crisis tend to be more open to faith as a means of comfort. Maybe this openness starts from a desperate place, but ask anyone whose loved one has crossed over or who experienced some awe-inspiring synchronicity at the moment they really needed a lifeline . . . they don't need science or validation from anyone else to know that what they felt brought some peace to their hearts. And that comfort can be a salve, often leading us to search for wider, more open horizons. At least that's what's happening for me.

CARING FOR YOUR SPIRIT & DEVELOPING FAITH

Perhaps you were raised with a strong faith, or you had more of a creative, free-range childhood that sparked lots of questions, like mine. Either way, if you've ever felt like an oddball, skeptic, or spiritual misfit (more wood nymph, less devout), you're not alone. My advice to us:

Stay wild: Staying wild means trusting your innate instincts and developing your intuition—the intelligence of your heart. Honoring your deep sensitivity and empathic abilities—your gift for reading and feeling energy. Regularly restoring and recharging yourself in nature and with animals. Staying open and receptive to the seen and unseen love that's ever present from many sources. And knowing that what you believe or don't believe has no bearing on who you are. Judgment is an overused human construct. We're all doing the best we can.

I love how Elizabeth Gilbert describes what she calls the "always life." After her partner died of pancreatic cancer, she explained that Rayya (her beloved) was still very present within her: "She's braided into me. I'm very comfortable saying, if nothing else, her afterlife is living within me, changing me, walking through the world with me and making me different. But I don't pretend to know much more than that." Amen, Liz.

After my dad died, my willingness to consider faith grew. It was that smile that spread over my dad's face as he passed into the next world that encouraged me in a way that words never could. I also turned 50, more years behind me than in front of me. More people dying and chapters ending. And so I surrendered my need for anything to make sense. I surrendered to comfort—and there's surely no downside to that.

Ask for a specific sign: Two years after Dad died, my best friend, Marie Forleo, invited me to a weekend workshop with psychic medium Laura Lynne Jackson. Ever wise, Marie knew I would benefit from learning how to connect with Dad and other loved ones who had passed. Laura encouraged us to ask for specific signs from loved ones and suggested we pick unusual ones, as an added way to bolster our faith. This made sense. I mean, picking a squirrel is kinda easy. Why not give the dead a harder job to do. So I picked a narwhal—a cross between a whale and a unicorn, with its long, spiraled tusk jutting from its head. If Dad could send me one of those, I was a believer.

Days went by . . . no narwhal. A week went by; where was my frickin' narwhal? Just when I was about to chalk it all up to nonsense, I walked into an antique store and right over the counter was a vintage print of a narwhal.

> "They can't pick up the phone and call us," says Jackson . . . "They can't put their arms around us and hug us. But they can find ways to do the symbolic equivalent of those things and let us know that they are with us. And when you have that experience, when you get that sign, it becomes a truth to you and it changes the way you're living: You know that death does not exist except for the physical and that you have a team of light rooting for you, supporting you, and guiding you at all times."

Turn your life into a treasure hunt: Pain may be loud, but reassurance is quiet. It waits for us to be aware. So whether you're in a season of grief or peace, turn your life into a treasure hunt. Look for signs each day of the ways you are being offered love, joy, peace, and reassurance.

Look for how you've grown during this time, how your heart has expanded and your wisdom has enriched you. Look for the continuity of the love. It's still there. The goodness is still with you, just as real and sacred as the grief. You just have to keep searching for signs and say a silent *Thank you* whenever you see them.

CHAPTER 9

Awkward Times, Awkward People

In times of stress, the best thing we can do
for each other is to listen with our ears and our
hearts and to be assured that our questions
are just as important as our answers.

— MR. ROGERS

Awkward times create awkward people—including you. Whether you're dealing with a full-blown crisis or you're trying to pick up the pieces after a significant loss, there are bound to be awkward and disorienting moments with those in your circle. They will say unbelievably weird and cringey things, and you will respond in weird and cringey ways too. You'll feel discomfort when you have to ask for help because your normal bandwidth for managing life is compromised. And you'll endure the rawness that comes from being out in the world while your heart is bleeding.

When we're in the midst of intense change, our interpersonal exchanges are subject to change, too. The rupture gives familiar dynamics the heave-ho—cue the awkwardness. But it also provides opportunities to get comfortable with discomfort. To learn new ways to express ourselves and our needs. Yay! (Just what you wanted.)

This chapter, filled with tips and real-world scenarios, is meant to help both people who are grieving as well as those who love and care for them. My hope is that we all emerge feeling a little more prepared, a little less awkward, and a lot more forgiving—of ourselves and each other.

I KNOW YOU MEAN WELL, BUT . . .

Don't be surprised if people do or say weird, totally confounding shit when your world falls apart. These well-meaning folks are often referred to as "grief illiterate." This doesn't mean they're jerks (although it may feel like it in the moment); it just means that they're inexperienced in handling the big emotions that accompany life's scary moments.

As we've well established, none of us were taught how to survive storms of this magnitude. You likely didn't know how to, either, before this sad, bad, mad, exhausting thing happened, and then it was trial by cancer, divorce, death, or some other flavor of crisis.

Let's be real, it's frickin' hard to know what to do or say when someone you love is in pain. It's also hard to know and ask for what you need when you're the one who's struggling. And because this rocky terrain is rarely traversed, it's easy to slip and unintentionally do or say insensitive things.

In my first book, *Crazy Sexy Cancer Tips*, I called the unconscious (and often insanely inappropriate) things people would say "cancer faux pas." Stuff like, *How long do you have to live?* or *My cousin got that and died.* Super comforting (and absurd), right?

Well, grief faux pas are just as common, if not more so. Pain has the power to turn us into Pez dispensers of tactless behavior. We fidget, fumble, and vomit out words that are never supposed to go together, because we're wildly insecure and uncomfortable.

A sample of grief-illiterate comments follows. Feel free to play along at home, adding any you might have heard, as well:

- *He's in a better place now . . .*
  (A better place is with me!)

- *It's God's plan . . .*
  (The God you're talking about sounds like a psychopath.)

- *You're young; you'll have another baby . . .*
  (I want *this* baby!)

- *Aren't you over it yet? It's been months, years, decades . . .*
  (I'm sorry I'm not as bounce back–y as you. There's no over; there's only through.)

- *At least she lived a long life . . .*
  (There is no such thing as "at least" in grief.)

- *There's a reason for everything . . .*
  (Excuse me while I vomit in my mouth.)

- *He really brought this on himself (smoked, drank, ate sausage, didn't call his mother on Sundays) . . .*

    (Fault and blame are toxic. Please don't.)

- *I know exactly how you feel . . .*

    (No, you don't. You know your experience of grief, but you don't know mine.)

- *There are other fish in the sea . . .*

    (I don't want fish. I want my person.)

- *It didn't happen to you, it happened for you . . .*

    (I just barfed in my mouth again.)

- *Why aren't you crying?*

    (Why are you judging me for how I grieve?)

- *It was only a dog; why are you so sad?*

    (Because my dog is my child to me.)

- *You're so strong . . .*

    (True. But it's exhausting to feel like I have to be.)

- *Well, I've been through worse . . .*

    (This isn't a competition, cookie.)

- *Let me know what you need . . .*

    (I'm already in decision fatigue. Just drop off a damn casserole.)

Scanning this list, you can see how attempts to connect with someone in their grief can unintentionally create more distance between you. Building on what we already know about grief illiteracy, let's break down some of these common missteps even further.

Denial. Another way we unconsciously screw things up is by putting our heads in the sand and pretending grief doesn't exist. *La, la, la, I can't hear you.* Nope. Take your fingers out of your ears, grief's still there. To be fair, maybe we're afraid to bring up whatever happened because we don't want the person to be reminded of their sorrow. Basically, we're worried we'll get it wrong, so we freeze.

Unfortunately, the person needing support doesn't always know how to interpret our absence; all they experience is more loss and isolation. Plus, those in grief or life shit pickles are all too reminded of their sorrow. We remember who and what we lost and when. Naming what has happened can potentially *help* the person struggling, especially when that acknowledgment is made with tenderness.

Centering ourselves. This happens when we hijack the conversation, center our own stories of grief, and shut the other person down: "Well, when my mom died . . . I lost my job . . . My ex-husband started dating our neighbor (I never trusted that sneaky woman) . . ." All of this causes the person who is grieving to feel unimportant and invisible. Your story matters, too. But their story matters more right now.

In the early days of my illness, I often found myself comforting friends who were having a tough time processing *my* difficult news. One person literally burst into tears when I told her the diagnosis. "Life is so unfair! And OMG, if this could happen to *you*, it could happen to *me*, too!" Oy vey. I'm exhausted just thinking about it.

The teachable moment. This is a favorite of those of us who skew cerebral. When the mere thought of emotion sends us into panic, we go to where we feel safest: what we've learned in books. Examples of this include masking our own discomfort by aggressively spouting unsolicited advice or telling you the lesson in all of this. While we're trying to be helpful, sometimes it's just awkward.

Look, it's a bird! We may also try to suppress our own legitimate pain by quickly changing the subject. For example, if we don't address our dying family member's concerns (their end-of-life planning, final wishes, and who gets the good china), maybe everything will be just *fine. Can we talk about something more positive, please?!* But what we're doing in these scenarios is denying the person a chance to unburden themselves and connect with us while they still have time to communicate.

And it's not just those who are dying who may need to talk. The same goes for those who have lost their loved one or are in the midst of another kind of crisis. *Your husband was arrested for a DUI? Wow, can you believe this weather?* The effect here is the same. By cutting off these conversations, you could be denying the chance to engage with your loved one around something that may truly matter to them.

Minimizing. Or we deny, dismiss, or downplay the situation in an attempt to get things "back to normal." *Why are you making such a big deal out of this? You're going to be fine.* Maybe, maybe not. People who sustain the emotional equivalent of a gaping wound don't feel fine. Insisting otherwise could feel like gaslighting. We would never do that intentionally, but regardless, the effect sucks. The message the person who's grieving may receive is that their feelings are immature or illegitimate, leading to self-doubt and possibly shame for feeling the way they do.

And then there are the *Whoa-did-that-really-just-happen* doozies. Grief faux pas that are so absurd, all you can do is laugh.

On the morning of Dad's celebration of life, one of his buddies FaceTimed my mom *at 3:30 A.M.* Nothing good happens at 3:30 A.M., folks. When the phone rings at that hour, someone is dead or in jail. In this case, Dad's pal just wanted my mom to know that she and I "don't look good." Over a hundred people were traveling from around the country to honor Dad, and apparently we needed to doll up better. The last time I checked, funerals weren't beauty pageants.

If you've ever been on the receiving end of any of these grief faux pas, you know how easy it is to think of these folks as unempathetic space aliens, but research actually shows quite the opposite. Observing someone else's pain sends a signal to our own brains, activating the same neural networks responsible for experiencing those same feelings, firsthand. It's as if the pain is somehow transferred, and when it hits our nervous systems, we instinctively freak out. And let's be real, freaked-out folks have a tendency to do fucked-up things—it's neurobiology, y'all!

In the end, there are no magic words that can take the pain away from those who are grieving or flailing in crisis. And it's not our job to do so—I can't emphasize this enough.

It's not your job to make it better. It's your job to bear witness, hold space for whatever feelings need to be expressed, and, above all, be loving.

Love always knows what to do.

COURAGEOUS ACKNOWLEDGMENT
(FOR THOSE WHO WANT TO OFFER SUPPORT)

As a person who has gone through grief in various forms, I've found courageous acknowledgment from the people around me, meaning addressing the elephant in the room, to be most helpful. Be willing to talk about what happened. Breathe and try to be good company to them (and to yourself). Can this be uncomfortable? Heck yes! Do it anyway. Remember, we're building valuable skills here. Skills we desperately need in the school of life. What you say—or don't say—carries a lot of weight. How you show up for those you love in times of need can strengthen your relationship or damage it.

Here are a few helpful ways to share your condolences:

- "I am so sorry you're going through this."
- "I'm not sure what to say, but I'm here to listen."
- "I don't know how you feel, but I'm here to help in any way I can."
- "I'm with you, and I love you."
- "I'll bet you could use some help right now. How about I . . . [fill in the blank—run errands, get you groceries, walk the dog]?"

Hug them. Hold their hand. Tell them you love them. Validate their feelings, especially the raw, embarrassing ones. Don't change the subject because you're sweating. Stay in the muck. Talk about the person they lost. Ask if they had any special birthday or holiday traditions together. Share good memories, especially ones they may not even know about. If you didn't know the person (or pet), you can say something like, "Though I didn't know him, I can only imagine how wonderful he was because *you* are so wonderful."

Send a text or leave a message letting them know you're thinking of them but that they don't need to respond. And don't take it personally if they don't. Take cues from them. If they don't want to talk, don't push. If they drop off the map, go find them. I have a tendency to isolate myself like a sick animal when my pain hits a tipping point (thanks, trauma). My closest true-blue friend, Marie, always catches the scent when I'm up to shenanigans like this. "Hey, just send me a smoke signal and let me know you're OK."

Proactively offer specific support (bring the lasagna, watch the kids, run errands, help with funeral arrangements—OMG, *please* help with those . . . that stuff is so hard). And don't just offer to help the week the loss happens. If you can, keep going, or at least keep checking in. Once the postdeath preparations, funerals, and celebrations of life are over, everyone else goes back to normal. But there is no normal for those left behind. Continuing to acknowledge the milestone dates (death anniversaries, birthdays, graduations) is the very definition of kindness.

Share and research resources, including the specific phone numbers and contact information (therapists, counselors, bodyworkers, or, if you're my crew, psychic mediums on speed dial). Give advice when appropriate and invited, but don't meddle or judge. *Huh? But how am I supposed to know the difference?* I get it. I'm a fountain of feedback, so this tip is really just for me (wink, wink).

Butting in on other people's business, when your participation isn't wanted, rarely feels good to them. Sometimes it can come off as shaming, corrective, or even patronizing, as if the other person is a dummy for not knowing.

Other times it might feel like you can't slow down enough to tune in to the person you're trying to help.

Again, if you're like me, giving unsolicited advice (even when it's great!) is as automatic and involuntary as breathing. In that case, you might say something like, "Do you want advice right now, or do you want to brainstorm, or do you just want to get it off your chest?" Asking permission never hurts. Remember, pain needs to be witnessed, not polished.

You can also be honest about your discomfort: "I don't know how to act and I'm afraid to get it wrong, but I love you and I want to try. Please tell me if I mess up." Then stay open to hearing what's helpful and what really isn't.

ACCEPTING HELP
(FOR THOSE WHO ARE GRIEVING)

I don't know about you, but I'm a master list maker. I have multiple "to-do" lists going at once, and I take great comfort each time I draw a line through a completed task. Sometimes I even add a task I've already done, just to have the satisfaction of the strikethrough. Well, for most of us, when we are grieving, list making and task blasting falls away and apart, deep into the abyss of grief, loss, and unwanted change. Our biggest goals for the day may just be to get out of bed and out of pajamas—the same ones we've been wearing for four days straight.

When we're hurting, we often hear the line "Please let me know how I can help." While it's a genuine and heartfelt overture, we're likely in no condition to provide friends and family with our daily/weekly schedule and details of our lives, even if we could use the help. This is where I suggest assigning one close friend (you know, the superorganized, bossy type) to field all the offers for help and organize and assign them into doable tasks. Whether it's walking a pet, picking up a prescription, grabbing groceries, driving kids to activities, dropping off meals, or even setting up an Amazon wish list, this person in command can be an invaluable resource for you. You may feel awkward about receiving this kind of support, but chances are, they are happy to be able to do some actual good. Take a deep breath and say yes.

If you're like so many of us, you may need to get over feeling like you're a burden to someone. Put yourself in their shoes. If the situation were reversed, you'd be right there offering practical or emotional support—gladly. Trust that those offering really *do* want to help. Just like you would want to help them. Think of it this way: Giving feels good. Don't rob the person of that feeling because accepting help is out of your comfort zone.

There are also going to be moments (lots of them) when you have no frickin' idea what you need, because you're overwhelmed. For such occasions, here are a few go-tos: "I'm not sure right now, but I could use a hug," and "I'm not sure right now, but could you ask me later in the week?" Then take a few moments to calmly reflect. It could be something as easy as "The next time you go to the store, would you mind grabbing some soup? I'm so not up to cooking right now."

One way or another, trust that support will find you when you need it most.

COCKTAIL PARTY RESPONSES

After a major life shake-up, going out and engaging in social situations can be tricky. We're already raw, and the prospect of having our wounds exposed is like getting an anxiety colonic. When I feel the need for protection, I make sure to have a few cocktail party responses in my back pocket, just in case someone asks me what is going on in my life.

"I haven't seen you in ages, what's new?"

What I want to say: "My dad's dead, my dog's dead, I feel dead!"

What I actually say: "It's been a rough few years, but I'm really looking forward to the holidays. Do you have any special plans?"

When I don't want to talk, I ask questions instead. It's a stealthy way to take the focus off me and direct it toward the other person. Because, sometimes we'd rather eat way too many passed hors d'oeuvres than open a can of anguish—and that's OK.

If it's not the time or place for a sensitive conversation, you can also just be honest and let the person know. My dad often handled this by saying, "Not right now." That was his way of letting us know that talking about whatever topic wasn't a no; it just wasn't a yes at that very moment.

And guess what? Not everyone needs to know your business. Distant colleagues, passing acquaintances, and anyone located several rungs outside your inner circle are on a need-to-know basis—meaning, you don't need to go there, especially if you're having a tender day. The deli guy, dry cleaner, mail carrier, and gal from accounting at your old job? Skip them.

SAY IT LIKE IT IS

There's something really liberating and honest about telling someone you're grieving. When they ask, "How are you?" you answer, "I'm sad." People don't admit that very often. But there's something innately human and empowering about dropping the mask (aka the mascara) and telling the plain ol' truth. Unfiltered honesty can feel like a dose of potent medicine for your healing.

Don't be surprised if your authenticity strikes a deep chord in the other person: "Me, too." This is an undeniable silver lining of your world falling apart: you're less inclined toward small talk, and more open to deeper intimacy. To recognizing that we're all just walking around with an assortment of boo-boos, longing for a place to belong.

Look, it's impossible to get all of this right. So, if you've ever been on either end of any of the awkward or painful behavior I've described, try to have compassion for yourself. We're all going to fumble and make mistakes, and that's OK. Own it, forgive yourself (and others—no one needs more baggage, this flight is full), and just keep trying.

CHAPTER 10

Love Is Love, Grief Is Grief

How lucky I am to have something
that makes saying goodbye so hard.

— WINNIE-THE-POOH

Grief is nothing if not humbling. We're forced to come face-to-face with our pain, in all its complicated, braided-together, grief-train glory, to reckon with the messy parts of ourselves that are not so attractive, like the judgments we sometimes harbor.

In grief circles, I've sometimes found that there's a lens through which our pain is filtered and even ranked. While there are certainly different degrees of complicated grief and tragic outcomes, one thing is clear: *you do you*. What other people think of your grief is none of *your* business; what matters is what *you* think. Whatever your heart is feeling matters.

As any pet owner who has mourned their beloved Fluffy heading over the rainbow bridge knows, the world is divided into two kinds of people: those who get it and those who don't. I was reminded of this when my dog Buddy died in 2016, just weeks before my dad was diagnosed with cancer. Buddy's loss felt as real as anything . . . because it was. Pain is pain.

With that in mind, this chapter is for anyone who's ever felt sheepish about grieving something deemed "not significant."

IN DOGS WE TRUST

While my great-great-grandfather put his bet on God, I choose dogs. Dogs (or any pets, for that matter) are our *chosen* family. They don't have the baggage that comes with actually being related to you. They don't ask you to drive them places and give them money. They don't marry deadbeats or leave their dirty underwear on the floor. And when you want to binge-watch *Judge Judy*, they're more than happy to join you—no complaints.

To them, you are Christmas morning. They're always ecstatic to be with you. Whether you've been gone for a week or you're just returning from changing a load of laundry, it's like, *OMG, you're back! It's sooo good to see you!*

Truth be told, sometimes I love animals more than people. Maybe it's because as a child, I had more four-legged friends than two-legged ones. Much to my mother's dismay, I was always rescuing critters. I even made outfits for my "guests" by cutting tail holes in my baby clothes—the ones my mom had meticulously saved for my own children.

Furry friends helped me through my tumultuous college years, painful breakups, job changes, and, of course, my diagnosis. My cat Crystal was the first "person" I uttered the "*c* word" to. ("It's cancer. What are we going to do, Crystal?")

Knowing that animals and nature would be a necessary part of healing my body, I left New York City after my diagnosis and moved to the mountains, where I dreamed of recovering and rescuing abandoned creatures in my spare time. Creatures who needed stable, loving homes—just like I once had.

But my attachment to my animals ramped up several notches when it became clear postdiagnosis that being a pet mommy was much safer than being a human mommy. If I wanted to mother a biological child, I might be putting my life at risk.

My oncologist described it like this: "Picture your disease like a rock balancing on top of a mountain. Right now, that rock is stable, not causing you any harm. If something (like the hormones from pregnancy) were to change that, your rock may start tumbling down the mountain. If that happens, there's a chance we can catch it. We just don't know if we can put it back on top of the mountain—which is where you're the safest. There are just too many unknowns, so think hard before you potentially wake the sleeping giant inside you."

Brian and I talked long and hard about this dilemma. Though we loved the idea of having kids, we weren't willing to put my life on the line to do it. Kids weren't a make-it-or-break-it part of our vision for a life well lived. Plus, the last thing I wanted was to abandon a child and a partner. I knew what growing up in an environment of absence and loss felt like, and I didn't want to pass that experience down the genetic chain.

Contemplating mortality helps you get real clear, fast.

We talked about adoption, but I was more open to the idea than Brian was—likely because I had such a positive experience with my own adopted father. Adoption isn't for everyone. It's also a lot harder for a stage IV cancer patient to qualify as a candidate. If my health deteriorated or I died, it would create more trauma for a kid who already experienced a painful and difficult start.

Together, we arrived at a place where we believed that while kids might have been an added joy, not having them didn't make us joyless or "childless" (such a belittling term). Quite the contrary. Our lives are filled with both joy and freedom. Brian and I are grateful for the time we have to explore our own desires, grow our relationship, and run an impactful business. We have amazing nieces and nephews, a hilarious godchild, and friends with adorable kids we love. We get to play and enjoy their curiosity, imagination, and priceless questions. We also get to leave and go out to dinner or watch a great movie when they melt down. Tantrums are our exit music.

But even though we've made peace and found a way to enjoy both worlds, we still needed to mourn this decision. We still needed to grieve our dreams of what might have been. And we still feel sad from time to time—all of which is normal. Plus, as much as I know everyone has their own baggage (which is more about them than me), I also still get hurt when I allow the occasional nasty comment from a random social media follower to burrow into my head.

Random follower (let's call her Betsy): "You'll never know real love if you don't have children."

Me: "Really, Betsy?"

Every human can know real love. Every single one of us. The humans with kids and the ones without them. Even the a-holes like Betsy.

LOVE COMES IN ALL SHAPES AND SIZES

Once we closed the door on the kids' chapter, I naturally poured my energy into my childhood love: animals.

Allow me to brag about my kids, like any proud parent.

My two great dog loves are Buddy and Lola. Buddy took after his father, Brian. Good-natured, even-keeled, and sweet. Lola was more like me, complicated. Lola was our planned child. A pit-bull mix who looked like a cross between a wild hyena and a Muppet. She was my writing companion, workout buddy, confidante, home security system, personal bodyguard, stylist (she preferred me in color, I like black), co-conspirator, best pal, and snug body pillow. Lola was also my soulmate.

Buddy, on the other hand, was an accident. I know you're not supposed to say that about your children, but it's true. One brisk fall day, Brian and I were on a hike in the Catskill Mountains. I'd been buttering him up to get another dog for months—Lola needed a sibling, after all—and the day of our hike, he'd finally agreed. As we made our way up the trail, we were excitedly making plans. "Can we go to the shelter later today to start looking? Should we get a boy or a girl? I like the name Star. Or Bowie. Or what about Buddy?"

That's when it happened.

We rounded a corner and there he was. A big, emaciated hound dog. Matted and covered in his own filth. We both instantly fell in love. From the start, Buddy was *ours*. Taking him home was a no-brainer.

With help from kind strangers we met along the way, we were able to get Buddy down the mountain, slowly and carefully. One hiker offered a blanket, another gave him part of his ham sandwich. Brian took off his belt and made a collar and leash. When Buddy looked like he needed a break, Brian carried him.

From that moment forward, they were inseparable.

Buddy came to us in bad shape—days away from dying. The vet told us that he was about 50 pounds underweight and very lucky to be alive. I scoured the local papers, Facebook posts, and lost pet registries, but could find no notice that anyone was looking for him. *Good!*

As we were trying to understand what happened to him, the vet explained that Buddy could have been dumped. His breed is often used for hunting, and this gentle fella was clearly no predator. Loud noises terrified him. He hated guns, thunder, and raised voices. When scared, he could snap, but most of the time, Buddy was mellow.

For months, we poured our hearts into healing our boy. We sprang into action researching the best diet, supplements, and holistic remedies. We made home-cooked food, tried herbal remedies, and even gave acupuncture a shot. Until he bit the vet. Apparently, needles were his red line.

When the weight wasn't coming on fast enough for his recovery, we added softball-size servings of raw ground beef to the mix. Twice weekly, this vegan would head to the butcher in a baseball hat and sunglasses. My love for Buddy knew no bounds.

Over time, Buddy transformed; he went from looking like he was at death's door to totally radiant. His matted coat became shiny, and his body functions normalized.

His spirit took longer to heal, though. Like all of us with wounds, his process couldn't be rushed. Buddy needed time, space, and stability until he felt safe enough to let his spark come back. Any sudden changes might trigger him. Once, I plopped down next to him on the sofa, unintentionally startling him awake. He instantly bit at the air like a great white shark leaping for a seal.

I got the message: "Be mindful around me; I'm still in a vulnerable state."

After a long and tender winter, Buddy's personality finally emerged. We were thrilled to meet the real him. Turns out, he was hilarious—a gentle, goofy giant, who went from being frightened of touch to moaning for ear noogies and full-body compression hugs.

When he wasn't holding court and welcoming visitors as the "mayor" of our porch, he was on patrol checking the perimeter and keeping us safe (or so we let him believe). Really, we were keeping him safe with our fenced-in yard and Garmin GPS collar. Our boy, with zero sense of direction, could really move, taking off like lightning—especially when a saucy squirrel was in his midst.

Buddy adored everyone, especially butterflies. He was an embodiment of love and reminded me a lot of my dad. Especially with how he handled what came next.

For a while, we chalked his weird gait up to a potential accident or issue from birth. His left leg made little half-moon circles when he walked, and he often stood like a ballerina (with his back legs in second position). Cute but odd.

We didn't think too much of it at first. But when his gait worsened, we took him to a specialist, where we learned that Buddy had degenerative myelopathy (DM), a disease similar to ALS in people.

Like ALS, there's no cure, and the end is, without fail, heartbreaking. Paralysis would eventually work its way through Buddy's body until he couldn't move or breathe, and there was absolutely nothing we could do about it. The vet gave him six months to live, tops.

No matter our family isn't daunted by chronic disease or so-called expiration dates. We knew we'd be able to give our boy the best, longest life possible. And that's exactly what happened.

As Buddy's disease progressed and he started to lose his ability to walk, we got him a wheelie cart (complete with trucker mud flaps), which he often flipped while chasing his little sister, Lola. When he stopped being able to relieve himself without assistance, we learned how to express his bladder and bowels. To say I'd be a good proctologist is an understatement.

We didn't think it was gross (OK, sometimes we thought it was *really* gross!), and neither did he. Right before each bowel expression, I'd sing, "Someone's knocking on the door, let me in, let me in." He'd dance, and I'd tickle a poop out. Sorry, I know this is really graphic, describing how I put my gloved finger in our dog's ass to stimulate a bowel movement, but this is a chapter about the unsung kinds of love—yours and mine. The shitty, totally embodied side of love that isn't always pretty, but is still very real. (And you thought my life was glamorous.)

But we also looked for signs from Buddy. Was this the life he wanted to live? The shitty thing about DM is that animals who have it are still fully themselves, even as their bodies are dying. Even though he was bedbound, he continued to take his job as mayor of the porch very seriously. He was still full of life and love and possibility—but his body was failing, and his time was slowly coming to an end.

We checked in with our vet, who reassured us that he didn't think it was time yet. He also praised our efforts and reassured us that it was OK to let go if we couldn't handle the care anymore. No, we told him, we could.

Then one day, he was ready.

Though we had some damn good times in those last months, Buddy started letting go. I watched as he retreated back to the internal cocoon-like state he was in when we first found him. His spark was replaced by anxiety and frustration. He had had enough. It was time.

That afternoon we made a love fort out of pillows in the middle of the living room. We held Buddy close and told him how much we loved him. Right before he passed, with the help of our wonderful vet, he popped his head up and looked straight into my eyes. In that moment, I felt his immense love, gratitude, and full presence. Then he peacefully left his body.

In the end, Buddy lived a year and a half longer than the vets expected, a year and a half of more love. He was a light when we grappled with our own big questions and made peace with our answers.

Loving Buddy was some of the best loving I've had the opportunity to experience. He helped us create our unique pack. He reminded us to champion our sensitivity and let our personalities shine—at our own pace. He showed us a greater capacity for love. And he reminded us that all beings deserve a chance to live the one life they've been given.

Love comes in all shapes and sizes. Little bundles of joy, big furry hound dogs, and scrappy beautiful mutts.

GRIEF IS GRIEF

The bond between animals and their humans is real, so when an animal dies and their daily dose of unconditional love becomes a memory, it's brutal. After Buddy died, Brian and I were devastated. Our boy was gone. The porch had no mayor. The air in our house was thick with sadness. Lola sat by the front door, waiting for Buddy to come home. He wasn't coming, though. As with all grief, the only way out was through.

Unfortunately, a lot of the grief literature and resources out there often overlook pet loss, or pay minimal lip service to it. But our furry, feathered, and scaly babies deserve better. And so do we.

I recently read a book that lists an actual "hierarchy of grief," as if the excruciating ache of loss can be simplified into neat categories of "importance." The fur mama in me was not having it when I saw animals listed on a lower rung (parents, too . . . really?).

I gotta be honest, though, as upset as I was—I know how deeply my heart ached after Buddy died—I also felt a little shame as I briefly internalized this hierarchy, considering this guideline for what and who *I* should (and should not) be grieving, and to what extent. So I decided to do some digging—did others feel the same?

Quite the contrary, I found plenty of folks who felt just like me: alienated. Many bristled at the idea that the loss of a pet (or grandparent) was somehow lesser. One woman shared how the loss of her dog brought up other, old grief, too. *The grief train.*

These sentiments were upsetting but also validating. When Buddy died, I wanted people to bring us lasagna; thankfully I have friends and family who did. In fact, my mother brought *all* the Italian food in the state of Connecticut. But people don't always think to do that when a pet dies. The loss isn't considered grief-y enough to warrant comforting Italian dishes.

As any devoted pet parent knows, losing a pet can be just as painful as losing a person. Losing a parent can be just as devastating as losing a partner. It doesn't matter that they may have "lived a long life." The same is true for a grandparent. It's not childish to be shattered when you lose your elders, no matter how old you are. (And no matter how old they are, either . . . a hole in your universe is a hole in your universe.)

The idea that I should be able to get over my grief more easily for my grandma, who died two weeks after I was diagnosed, or my dad, because these losses are inevitable—expected even, and therefore less traumatic—is just not true. The same is true for miscarriage. You're not "overreacting" if you're devastated. The moment you decided to conceive your connection began. Just as there is no hierarchy of love, the same is true of grief. Instead, grief is shaped by what someone or something meant to you.

So if you've ever felt shame or judgment around your grief, like you're just being a big baby for feeling it—or worse, like there's something pathologically wrong with you—I'm hugging you from afar. In my experience, when people judge you, it's a reflection of their own wounds and fears, not you.

Remember, you don't need permission to feel your big feelings, for as deeply or as long as you need to. From my big grieving heart to yours, you feel what you need to feel for whatever and whoever has left your world. I'm a grown-ass woman. I'm a feeler. I'm sensitive. I love fully when I love. And damn it, I really miss my dog.

CHAPTER 11

SELF-CARE IN THE STORM

I have come to believe that caring for myself is not self-indulgent. Caring for myself is an act of survival.

— AUDRE LORDE

Self-care is usually the first thing to fall by the wayside when we're in crisis. We're taking care of our family, friends, career, home, pets, finances, community, and more. Oftentimes we're last on the list. And if, by some chance, we're able to carve out a wee bit of space for ourselves, we may not know where to start or what to do. Perhaps it's been so long since we've filled our own tank it feels impossible. *Why bother?*

Here's why: because when we're not OK, self-care is *exactly* what we need.

In difficult times, you're inevitably going to be more depleted, which means it's important to be intentional about how you use and replenish your energy. Nurturing yourself, in even the smallest ways, will help you become more stress-hardy.

But I know this is easier said than done. As we delve into the topic of self-care, allow me to point out the obvious: For more than two decades, I've made my living as an internationally known wellness expert. If there's one thing I know, it's the ins and outs of self-care. But when crisis hits, what we know goes flying out the window.

At various rupture points, I'd find myself passing up a walk in nature, opting to stay completely glued to my phone, doom scrolling or devouring celebrity gossip. Or zoning out with endless TV and eating cereal for dinner (more nights than I'd like to admit). During these times, my connection to self was nowhere to be found. Sound familiar?

In this chapter, I'm going to walk you through some essential self-care basics. (Clearly, I could use a reminder, too.)

But let's get one thing clear: no one is expecting you to embark on a full-blown lifestyle makeover. Setting the bar that high is not only a recipe for burnout, it will likely backfire. Instead, just let my words soak in. When you're ready, I encourage you to choose *one* simple action you can take to help yourself feel better. Just one. After you've got some consistency under your belt, add another.

Above all, let it be easy. You're already doing enough hard stuff. This is meant to nourish you, not send you over the edge.

DO AS I SAY, *NOT* AS I DO

For me, cleaning is a contact sport. When life feels groundless, I grab some Windex and wipe the shit out of it. Cleaning with gusto makes me feel accomplished. There's a clear beginning, middle, and end. No mystery. No uncertainty. No "better luck next time." Only a satisfying sense of completion. The floor was dirty. The floor is now clean. Cue the trumpets!

A year after Dad died, I decided that my staycation was the perfect time to "tackle" my back-burner to-do list. Not the doctors' appointments I'd neglected to make or the teeth cleaning that was long overdue. Instead, I went for the unimportant stuff that eats at you in the early-morning hours when you're trying to get back to sleep but can't because you own expired spices, socks with no mates, and piles of rotting paperwork. How are you expected to rest?

And what about those freaky Halloween decorations that Mom *keeps* sending you, or your collection of VHS tapes? The '90s called and they want their VCR back—get rid of them! (Well, except for the *Buns of Steel* workout video. That's a classic.)

So, you must attack these offensive objects. Seize your few-and-far-between moments of energy, throw your hair into a struggle bun, and vigorously declutter your environment—channeling all your anxiety, stress, and hopelessness into the organization of stuff.

I was barely a few hours into my compulsive purge-a-thon when . . . *crunch!* My back went out. Brian had tried to stop me: "Babe, be careful, that's *really* heavy. Let me help you." No. I insisted on lifting it myself, because why accept help (or your own limitations) when you can push and force? Why not lift heavy things by yourself?

It's what you've done emotionally most of your life, taking everything on with a cheery smile. (You should have *I'm fine, damn it* tattooed on your forehead.) And for the love of God, why remember that you are a couch potato, and tubers like you have no business impersonating CrossFit champs? Sigh.

Unfortunately, I am still unable to answer most of those questions.

My friend Wayne Muller, author and minister, captures my cleaning mania beautifully: "We take refuge in speed, we avoid the searing burning in the heart by chasing swiftly this way and that, we become a moving target, so it is more difficult for those unbearable feelings to find us. We refrain from rest, refuse to even pause. Faster feels better because it allows us to avoid accepting what we need."

When I'm trying to outrun my feelings, that's *exactly* what I do. I give what energy I have to others or to my work, and if there's any left, I tidy, I clean, I move at a supersonic pace to avoid myself. Maybe you can relate.

But you know what helps me stop (beside back pain?): understanding what my body needs and why. Though it may not always feel like it, our bodies do so much for us while asking for little in return. Let's get to know our beautiful beings a bit more. Doing so may reinspire you to care for yourself.

TEND TO YOUR GARDEN

Your body is an extraordinary ecosystem, and you are the custodian of your delicate inner terrain. Pretty amazing, right? Take a moment and visualize this with me. Imagine that inside your body, there's a beautiful garden. A lush space full of all kinds of budding life—all working in harmony.

Standing in that garden, we begin to realize that there's no single choice that's going to determine whether it's healthy or not. Instead, there are dozens of factors that make a difference: the quality of the soil, the quality of the water, whether there's enough sunlight, the presence or absence of pollutants, the presence or absence of nutrients, and so on.

Whether you're aware of it or not, there are dozens of decisions you make *every* day that help your garden either thrive or lose its vibrancy.

The scientific study of the choices and conditions that determine whether your garden thrives is called epigenetics. *Epi-* literally means "above." So these are the factors that have nothing to do with your genes but can still determine how they behave.

Now, it's true that your genes influence many aspects of your well-being. They're like the seeds that were planted in your garden long before you ever got there. You had no control over those early seeds. But thankfully, those inherited seeds don't have to determine your future. Your genes are not your destiny. Which is *why* self-care is health care—it's that important. Even more so when we're shells of our former selves.

Regardless of the DNA blueprint you were born with, you can help determine where your health goes from here. Once I learned about epigenetics, I never looked back. True, cancer was still in my body, but now I had an answer as to what I could do to help. I could create an environment in my body where cancer and other diseases were less likely to thrive and health was more likely to flourish.

People often ask me, "What's *one* thing I can do to support my health?" My answer is always the same, whether you're a patient or you hope to never become one: "Tend to your garden."

THE FIVE PILLARS OF WELLNESS

In my online community, I teach simple practices to support what I call the *Five Pillars of Wellness*: the five areas that will have the biggest impact on your well-being—body, mind, and spirit. I'm going to walk you through a condensed version of the pillars to help you jump-start your own self-care practice, but if you want to go deeper, or get coaching from me, go to my website (kriscarr.com) for more details.

The Five Pillars are as follows: being mindful of what you're *eating, drinking,* and *thinking,* and how you're *resting* and *renewing.*

I designed this holistic approach for one very important purpose—to combat the number one garden killer: inflammation. As you may know, chronic inflammation is like living in a constant state of fight-or-flight in your body. And it's often triggered by prolonged stress. If you're overburdened at work or carrying financial or family pressure; if you haven't been sleeping well for a long period of time; or if you're struggling to eat well, stay hydrated, and move your body, all of this can contribute to chronic inflammation. (And let's face it, we're under no greater stress than when we're grieving, missing a loved one, or otherwise trying to piece our fractured selves back together. That's why tending to your garden is extra important.)

Whatever the cause, that inflamed condition eventually stresses your system so much that it gets confused and starts attacking its own healthy tissue. The result is a slew of nasty symptoms, including chronic pain, joint stiffness, headaches, fatigue, loss of appetite, fever, and chills. Long term, it also makes us more susceptible to serious disease, including heart disease, diabetes, and cancer.

That's why caring for the pillars can help you so much right now.

Let's go through some simple ways to do that.

Pillar One—What You're Eating

When we're just trying to survive whatever storm we find ourselves in, it's easy to skimp on nutrition. Yet the more we shortchange ourselves, the worse we feel, and the tougher it becomes to get through the day and function at the levels a crisis demands.

The simplest thing you can do when you don't have much time or energy is to eat more plants. Despite all the conflicting information on nutrition, there's consensus: plants are *really* good for you. They're full of vitamins, minerals, enzymes, antioxidants, phytochemicals, fiber, and other important stuff that'll help your body function well and be resilient. Yet, according to the CDC, fewer than 10 percent of adults are getting their recommended daily allowance. Here's a sneaky solution to help you consume more plants.

Add Before You Subtract

This advice may sound counterintuitive, because most diet culture is driven by deprivation. Instead of stressing yourself out about what you can and can't have (because that rarely works), try a kinder approach: add before you subtract.

Adding more water will reduce the amount of soda you drink. Adding some fruit after dinner will reduce the number of cookies you eat. The more healthy stuff you add, the more crap you crowd out.

On your plate, this advice looks like fruits, veggies, whole grains, healthy protein sources, and good fats. Add at least one vegetable at each meal today. Make a smoothie for breakfast by adding a handful of greens to your favorite fruits. Add a side salad to your lunch. Heap on those greens at dinner, and so forth. Bon appétit!

Pillar Two—What You're Drinking (Time to Hydrate)

When you're dehydrated, your body just doesn't function as well. You can't properly metabolize carbs and proteins; it's hard to flush out waste products; and you can suffer from headaches, joint aches, brain fog, low blood pressure, fatigue, and more. This is why I'm so passionate about hydration. Titillating, I know.

Drinking enough water will not just help you feel better; it's *essential* for a strong immune system. And what takes a hit when you're going through a rough time? Your immune system. Stress, poor sleep, running on empty, and dehydration can all add up.

But, continuing our theme of adding before you subtract, I'm *not* going to tell you to cut things like coffee, cola, or sports drinks right now. You do you. Instead, I encourage you to up your water intake.

To figure out how much water you need, divide your body weight in pounds by two to get the approximate amount of water in ounces you need to drink per day. If you're using the metric scale, divide your weight in kilograms by 30 to determine how many liters of water you need. The water content from your fruits and veggies counts toward your daily intake—but don't worry about trying to calculate that. Also, some medical conditions require fluid restrictions, so do your research there.

Will you need to pee more? Yup. Think of it as if you're peeing your way to better health. Plus, every time you get up to "go" is another opportunity to get steps in—that's exercise!

Pillar Three—What You're Thinking (Stress Reduction, Please)

All the kale and water on planet Earth won't do diddly-squat if you're snorting lines of stress. That's why the thinking pillar is about supporting your mental health. Here are some suggestions to consider:

Start Your Day with "Thank You"

How we start our day sets the tone for how we'll end it. What if you took your first few moments, the time that bridges your dream state with your conscious mind, and just said *Thank you. Thank you, body. Thank you, spirit. Thank you, creator*—whatever feels right to you. *Thank you for another day. I am blessed.* It's natural to focus on what we don't have or what we've just lost. But gratitude reminds us of what's *still* good in our lives—and there is plenty.

Meditate for Just a Few Minutes

You don't have to hole up in an ashram to find still-ness. For most of us, that's both unrealistic and unappealing. And yet, meditation is an extremely beneficial practice, especially when you're hurting. The trick is to find what works for you. Don't worry if you think you're "bad" at it (no such thing) or if you have no idea what you're doing at first. Years ago, I took a workshop with one of my favorite teachers, Pema Chödrön. Pema is a Buddhist teacher and nun who's been meditating for more than 40 years. I nearly fell off my cushion when she joked about being terrible at meditating. If *she* claims to stink at it, you (and I) can stink at it, too. How well we meditate is not as important as our commitment to regularly calming our nervous system. Here's an easy way to start:

Sit in a comfortable position for 5 to 10 minutes and focus on your breath. When a thought comes (*I wonder if those shoes are on sale? Is that urine I smell on the carpet? When was the last time I shaved my legs?*), gently acknowledge the thought by silently saying "thinking" and then bring your attention back to your breath (without judgment).

You can also try counting. For example, silently count from 1 to 10 in your mind. When a thought interrupts you, stop where you are and go back to 1. Don't be surprised if you don't get far or if you suddenly wake up and find you're at 110! Another option is to silently repeat an affirmation like "I am love." The goal of these techniques is to use whatever you're focusing on (breath, counting, or affirmations) to anchor yourself to the present moment.

Take Brain Breaks throughout the Day

The last few years have been so intense that it's no surprise that your brain may feel like burned toast. While meditation, or any practice that soothes your nervous system, is important, your brain also needs breaks throughout the day. Pause. Step away from your computer. Breathe. Stretch your arms to the sky. Walk to the mailbox or the end of your block. Or if you're like me, lie on the floor and moan. Even just five minutes can help you recharge.

Talk to Someone

As we've explored, talk therapy can be a mental health lifeline (it certainly has been for me). If you don't have a therapist, counselor, or spiritual advisor, you may want to add one of these to your healing crew. Here are some resources to help you find someone to talk to (including telehealth and online sessions):

- *Psychology Today* has a directory of verified therapists on its website. You can put in your zip code to learn who's in your area.

- The **Anxiety and Depression Association of America** website also has a "Find a Therapist" section, as well as other resources for anxiety or depression.

- The **National Alliance on Mental Illness** allows you to access online support groups and other free mental health educational resources.

- **Better Help** is a good resource for online therapy. They offer text message support and phone or video sessions and have different levels of plans to meet your needs and budget.

If you're a therapy newbie or have struggled to find a good fit in the past, know that you are in the driver's seat. Though it's easy to put therapists up on a pedestal, they're human beings, too. If you're on the fence after the first meeting, reflect on why you're questioning this fit and raise these points with your therapist. How they respond will tell you a lot about whether or not they're the right person for you. If something in your gut doesn't feel right, don't dismiss it outright. At the end of the day, it's important to work with someone you feel comfortable going to uncomfortable places with.

Medication

When Dad became terminal, medication helped keep me from sinking under waves of depression. His loss felt too big to handle without completely losing myself. And yet, for years I was resistant to pharmaceutical intervention, even just as a bridge to get me to a steadier place. Medication, especially in the wellness world, is often stigmatized. Not surprisingly. The incidents of doctors overprescribing medications are well documented, and many medications carry unwanted, and often debilitating, side effects.

But medication wasn't new to me. It helped me through difficult periods at other times in my life, including when I started having panic attacks after meeting BD. So, I knew what chronic depression felt like, I'd experienced prolonged bouts of white-knuckling through it, and I could tell when I was sinking into it again. And yet it took me nine months of unbearable struggle before I was brave enough to meet with a psychiatrist and get my own prescription.

I was so relieved once I did. There's no shame in finding reasonable ways, including medication, to help navigate these kinds of highly emotional and upsetting situations.

Medication has helped me navigate my own grief and trauma. I never expect it to solve my problems or replace the hard and rewarding work of healing, but it has allowed me to stay buoyant when the ocean swells surround me. Everybody's journey is different and personal. I hope that by sharing my tools and experiences, you feel less alone.

Pillar Four—How You're Resting (The Health Benefits of Sleep)

When I talk with people about their biggest health challenges, sleep is often the number one issue. Most of us know how stressful it is to toss and turn all night, and many of us experience this on a regular basis. In America alone, 70 million people suffer from some sort of sleep disorder. Either folks aren't getting enough sleep, they're staying up too late or rising too early, or their sleep is so restless they wake up feeling exhausted.

When we're affected by grief, overwhelm, stress due to increased caregiving, prolonged worry, personal health issues, a global pandemic, toxic politics, social unrest, injustice, economic hardships, and so forth, sleeping well can feel impossible. But many major restorative functions occur while we sleep. For adults, the biggies are muscle growth, protein synthesis, and tissue and cell repair. For infants and children, hormone production and brain development are key (which is why they need so much more sleep than we do). For all ages, sleep is key to ongoing emotional regulation and processing as well. Dreams, too, can help in the processing of traumatic events. And it goes without saying that in difficult times, we need all the emotional support we can get.

Not getting enough sleep can negatively impact your mental health, memory, stress response, and more. It increases your chances of developing type 2 diabetes, heart disease, high blood pressure, stroke, and respiratory and metabolic disorders.

The number of hours needed is different for everyone, but 7½ to 8 hours usually does the job, with your most restorative window typically between 11 P.M. and 7 A.M. because your circadian rhythm is at its lowest point.

So with better sleep in mind, here are some ways to set yourself up for success:

Tuck Yourself in Like a Toddler

If you had a feisty four-year-old who needed to be asleep by 8 P.M., what time would you start getting them ready for bed? Probably not at 7:59 by shutting off whatever screen they have in front of their face and plopping them on the pillow. Instead, there'd be a soothing bath, teeth brushing, soft PJs, a bedtime story, maybe a nighttime prayer. All topped off with a kiss good night. Take a cue from the toddler plan, my friend. If you want to be asleep by 11 to get your 8 hours of shut-eye, that doesn't mean getting into bed at 11. Create a peaceful routine to ease yourself into rest instead. Plan to be in bed with your whole routine done at least 15 to 20 minutes before you'd like to be asleep.

Keep It Dark and Cool

Darkness stimulates natural production of melatonin, the hormone that helps you snooze, while light from digital clocks and devices tells your brain to rise and shine. That's why sleeping in a completely dark room is so important. A sleep mask or room-darkening curtains will help if you can't control your environment. When I travel, I put my T-shirts over any little light intruder. Keep your room cool, too, ideally between 60 and 67 degrees (15.5 and 19 degrees Celsius). It will help you avoid waking up in the middle of the night, kicking off the covers, and shouting, "I'm hot!"

Skip or Reduce Caffeine and Go Easy on the Alcohol

As you're likely well aware, caffeine makes it harder to fall asleep, but it doesn't stop there—it can also interfere with the *quality* of your rest. If you're having trouble getting or staying asleep, stick with decaf, herbal tea, or one cup of coffee early in the morning. And when it comes to booze, peel back and drink it earlier in the evening (with food and lots of water) or not at all. Alcohol feels like a sedative because it slows down motor and brain function, often leaving us relaxed. But as it's metabolized, it acts like a stimulant in our bodies. This is what wakes us up in the wee hours of the morning—the perfect time to ruminate about shit you do not need to be ruminating about at that moment.

Pillar Five—How You're Renewing (Movement)

Everyone I know wants to have more energy, especially when the going gets tough. But here's what most people don't understand: we have to expend energy to make it. Our cells contain little engines called mitochondria. They're responsible for turning our food into fuel. The quality and quantity of engines in our cells determines the quality and quantity of energy we have.

How to build these little suckers? Exercise. Exercise gives more energy than it takes. The more you move, the more mitochondria your body makes, and the more energy you will have. Not to mention better mood, healthier digestion, and stronger immunity. But what if you're too tired? Start small. Even just 10 minutes of movement per day (walking, aerobics, dance—anything you love that gets your heart pumping) significantly reduces stress and anxiety and supports your physical well-being.

THE FIVE PILLARS IN ACTION

Give yourself a pat on the back, my friend. You made it through the Five Pillars. When you're feeling drained or immobilized by life's ruptures, a little bit of effort can go a very long way.

Before we move on, take a moment to reflect on what we just explored. When you're ready, just choose *one* self-care practice to start exploring right away. Here are some examples.

Maybe you opt for a side of broccoli instead of fries. Order green juice instead of coffee, herbal tea over your nightly Manhattan. Give yourself even five minutes in the morning to set a positive intention for your day. Tend to your nighttime sleep routines with a bit more loving care, turning your phone off and the binaural beats up. Take the stairs instead of the elevator, and work simple stretching into your daily routine.

I promise you, small steps are your friend. We're rebuilding. Replenishing. Regenerating. And we're doing it in thoughtfully paced ways that avoid overwhelm and more despair.

Got it? Good job.

CARE FOR THE CAREGIVER

Raise your hand if your caregiving instincts have been on overdrive for longer than you can remember. You're not alone. While much of this next section focuses on the demands of caring for a loved one who is sick, a lot of these same sentiments apply to caregiving in other kinds of crises. If being superhuman and helpful is your default mode, this is for you.

From the day he was diagnosed to the day he died, my dad's cancer journey was profoundly more meaningful, joyful (certainly more organized)—and yes, longer—thanks to the steadfast support he got from my mom. She was a walking masterclass in how to show up for someone, day in and day out, in ways big and small. But I also watched as it impacted her own well-being and sense of self over those five years.

The constant demands of caring for a person who has a serious illness can really take a toll because the level of need is so high and often all-consuming. You're juggling doctors' visits; medical note taking; administering doses of medicine; fielding visitors; communicating the latest health status with relatives; making sure there's enough water, tissues, and food handy . . . all while staying on heightened alert for any emerging needs or symptoms you've not encountered before. It's no wonder that, according to caregiver.com, between 40 and 70 percent of caregivers suffer from depression, while many also have anxiety and all the stress that comes with it.

For some, the lack of boundaries between their roles as a caregiver and spouse, child, or other loved one can be extra challenging. You're the loving wife, but you also have to play medicine sheriff. You're the loyal cousin, but you also have to act as a personal assistant, helping your loved one stay on top of appointment details. Navigating dual roles (and tasks) is something we do out of love and sometimes necessity. I say "sometimes" because it's possible that we are so blinded with panic that we don't realize we could actually ask for help. We think we're the only ones who can handle the big stuff, when in reality that might not be true.

Caregivers often put unrealistic expectations on themselves, trying to do it all and neglecting to let others know when they're drowning. Sometimes, that's because making a specific request for assistance can feel like too tall an order—that would mean pausing long enough to even think. Other times, we don't ask because we don't want to be a burden on anyone, or maybe we've made the determination that our needs are less important.

My friend Liz had been keeping vigil for weeks at her sister's hospital bed, when an unexpected comment finally got her to pay attention to her own self-care. When Liz wasn't with her sister, she was fielding anxious calls and texts from her sister's friends. After one friend asked her for emotional support, she naturally obliged.

"Wow, it's unreal how you're able to take care of her *and* all of us, too," the friend said. To Liz, this praise was no gold star. It was a wake-up call.

Liz had been moving so fast and juggling so much that she didn't realize how her own grief and anxiety had turned her into a nonstop supergiver. From then on, Liz was more mindful of what she could and couldn't handle. She asked close friends to keep her honest and help brainstorm areas she might be able to advocate for more support.

If you're anything like Liz, accepting help can be hard when *you* are the person everyone comes to, not the other way around. I'm a caregiver for my illness, my family, my friends, my business, my community. And I'm good at it. But these last few years have shown me how easy it is to revert back to self-abandoning behaviors when I'm anxious, depressed, or just plain overwhelmed.

While you may believe that *you've got this*, you can't handle it *all* on your own (nobody can).

If you're actively caring for a sick or dying loved one, or a loved one with disabilities, I encourage you to set up some much-needed respite care for yourself. Take breaks. Reach out to family members and friends for help.

Depending on your resources, a home-health nurse, adult-care programs, meal-delivery services, a cleaning person, or even a personal assistant can help you carry the load. A good resource to check out is care.com.

If money is tight, consider doing a swap with some-one. Maybe you can make some extra meals in exchange for something you need. With a little research, you might find free or low-cost services in your area. Contact your local hospital to see if they know of specific support resources in your area; they often do.

And when you have those breaks . . . use them to take care of *yourself.* Make your own doctors' appoint-ments, schedule time with a therapist, get a manicure, or just take a nap.

For as long as I can remember, I preferred giving rather than receiving. Giving made me feel less vulnera-ble. If I was the giver, nothing could be taken from me. I didn't have to worry if I could trust someone. If I didn't receive, I couldn't fall short of expectations. Beliefs like this make it hard to create close relationships and easy to burn out.

If you find yourself in a season of life where you are doing the lion's share of caregiving, this is your friendly reminder that you can channel some of that beautiful lov-ing energy toward yourself, too.

And finally, even if the eye of the storm is behind you, you still need self-care—maybe even more so. There's a reason we get sick after big projects, in the wake of life changes, and postcrises. It's as if our bodies finally have time to exhale (and fall apart). Keep tend-ing, my friend.

RAISE YOUR STANDARDS FOR THE PEOPLE IN YOUR LIFE (AND LOWER THEM FOR YOURSELF)

People-pleasing, aka wanting to make everyone around you happy (or just not annoyed that you have needs, too), is one of the biggest energy saboteurs. I know it can be a hard habit to break, but I invite you to be more discerning about where you put your precious energy. Some folks really drain you. When I'm out of sorts, I need to have high standards for the people I allow in my inner circle. If I'm running on empty, no energy vampires allowed.

What about partners, parents, and kids? They can certainly suck the life out of us from time to time—even when they don't mean to. This is where boundaries come in. It's OK to communicate your limits. There's a fantastic word that will help you do that. Ready for it? *No.* (It's a complete sentence.) Go ahead and take it for a spin. I promise you can handle it.

Encouraging others to be more self-reliant serves us all. Honesty works, too. "I'd really love to come to your work function, but I'm too spent. Rain check for a time when I'm not so depleted?"

I'm not suggesting that you let your toddler or elderly parent fend for themselves. I'm merely pointing out that there are probably some tasks that people can do on their own. Making a sandwich doesn't require a Mensa membership.

And not for nothing, but there are also a few folks in your life who probably take more than they give. Now is a good time to start adjusting that balance.

GIVE YOURSELF A PASS

You're not going to be able to have your shit together all the time. Not when you're maneuvering through the kind of turbulence that requires barf bags. This is where the saying "progress, not perfection" comes in. Perfection sucks the life force right out of you. It kicks your batteries in the balls. Ouch! Don't do that.

Instead, let your new self-care mantra be this: "It's good enough."

Good enough creates momentum. Good enough allows you to implement better habits. Good enough keeps you from quitting on yourself. Good enough is likely all you've got right now, and, well, it's good enough.

You're going to disappoint people. (It's good enough.)

You won't be able to pick up the phone as much. (It's good enough.)

You'll forget to RSVP, and you'll cancel plans at the last minute. (It's good enough.)

Your e-mail inbox will get so bad that you may decide to declare e-mail bankruptcy, delete everything, and start again. (It's good enough.)

You won't be the best friend or the greatest parent or partner right now. (It's good enough.)

You won't "look so good." (It's good enough—and so are you.)

You'll need to cut yourself some slack. (It's good enough.)

Now, go get a glass of water, my friend. Cheers.

CHAPTER 12

LISTENING TO YOUR LIFE

Listen to your life. See it for the fathomless
mystery that it is. In the boredom and pain of it no
less than in the excitement and gladness: touch,
taste, smell your way to the holy and hidden heart
of it because in the last analysis all moments are
key moments, and life itself is grace.

— FREDERICK BUECHNER

Here we are in the final chapter, and yet, there's no
finality to grief, trauma, and loss. There's reaching new
stages of healing, but as we all know, those old feelings can
still erupt like geysers when we least expect it.

While there may be no getting over grief, there is
moving forward. There is moving through. And no matter
what your situation, there will be a moment when you
breathe and think, *OK, I'm here now. What's next?*

TAKING INVENTORY

When things fall apart, there's often a domino effect—a chain reaction sparked by the initial rupture. Facing death shows us the other parts of our lives that are dying, too. Our outworn patterns, partnerships, and parts come into sharp focus. This trickle-down effect makes perfect sense. All systems of life are interconnected, and what isn't working in one area often illuminates the struggle in other areas, too.

When life gets upended, some corner of our psyche becomes more aware that we will one day leave this planet. No one really wants to think about that (including me). But perhaps the heightened awareness of our limited time helps us see more keenly which parts of our lives could be pruned to make space for our next chapter. I think back to David Kessler and what he said about how, when our loved ones are nearing the end of their lives, we have to "ride the damn horse in the direction it's going." Just as that's a sobering metaphor for the dying, it also applies to the parts of ourselves that have died (or are dying) in the process of loss and crisis. When we resist the undercurrent of deep inner transformation, we're also resisting the natural growth process.

In retrospect, the dominoes that fell once Dad got sick now seem inevitable, like they had been a long time coming. My mind always goes back to the conference I spoke at in 2016, before the return flight was delayed, before Mom greeted me at the door at midnight, before the words "Dad has a mass on his pancreas" changed our lives forever. Readying myself to go onstage that night to hopefully inspire people to live fully, I remember thinking, *Once this is over,* then *I'll live.* Once *this* task—obligation, deadline, to-do—was complete, *then* I'd [take better care of myself, visit my best friend . . . fill in the blank].

But every time I finished a task or project, I failed to pause and keep the promises I had made to myself. Instead, I'd automatically turn to another item on my list. I knew I needed to recalibrate for quite some time. I just didn't know how.

Then illness happened, loss happened, crisis happened, and once again, I was reminded that life is always speaking to us. At first, it taps us gently and whispers in our ears. Our intuition sharpens and our gut tingles. Our dreams become more vivid as we unconsciously work out the messages being offered in our sleep. Life continues trying to get our attention in the hopes that we'll recalibrate on our own.

But when we refuse to pick up what life is laying down, those whispers can turn into wrecking balls. It's kinda like the Glenn Close character in the movie *Fatal Attraction*. Life basically says, "I will not be ignored, Dan." And if you shrug her off long enough, she'll boil your bunny. Horrific, I know. Maybe your life isn't as deranged (and dramatic) as mine, but my point still remains: Don't blow off the messages. Listen to the whispers before they become roars.

Even though it's human nature to kick the can down the road because fear comes up, excuses multiply, and there's a sale at Target, life (like Glenn Close) is very persistent.

So what then? And what if change takes time (which it certainly can)? Well, sometimes I think it might be enough to simply take note: *I see you, Glenn. I see you, life.* But at some point, you will be called to take action to listen to your heart. To listen to life.

Losing Dad was a rupture so all-encompassing that I couldn't just pick up the pieces and move forward with business as usual. The pieces no longer fit. I could no longer rely on sheer will to survive. I'd developed the skills that got me to a certain place in my health, marriage, and career, but I knew they couldn't get me through this next chapter. Faith was the only answer. Not necessarily in God—though I was certainly more open than ever to divine support—but rather faith in listening to and trusting myself.

Sometimes things fall apart, and it's completely out of our control. Other times things fall apart because they need to. That doesn't always mean that the relationship or job (or whatever) needs to end, but it does mean that change is already on the way, whether we like it or not. Scary, I know.

For me, what needed to change was my relationship to my work. As I've shared, I used to bury myself in "busy" because I didn't know any other way. Next, I hustled hard because I loved the praise it got me. Later, I grinded because it was a great way to avoid big feelings. When I noticed a "disturbance in the force" like, say, grief, I knew exactly how to swat it away. Get busy—emotions averted, deadlines met. *Winning!* Or so I thought.

I wish I could have gently coached myself the way I would have a member of my community. But often it's easier to see the wounds, fears, and perceived limitations that drive others than it is to connect to these parts of ourselves.

In truth, every coach needs a coach, and my coach was gone. Dad had always guided me through big life transitions. I'd lay out my thoughts or problems with him, even the stuff I didn't want to admit, and no matter how gnarly my dilemma, he'd help me find a path forward by saying the things I needed to hear, like . . .

"Don't hold back."

"Dig deep and hold fast."

"Say 'I love you.'"

"Let yourself off the hook."

"Show up."

"Make it a great day."

And even, "Knock it off." An oldie but goodie that snaps me out of brain rot.

His business advice, in particular, was often applicable to other areas of life, too. He'd remind me to "do the hard thing first," which sometimes meant making the hard call, tackling the annoying job, and getting the tough stuff behind me without delay. Every time I've followed his guidance, I inevitably feel a weight lifting off my chest, even when it was a task from hell.

Another one of his gems was to encourage me to ask myself the candid question I often didn't want to even think about: *Have I reached the point of diminishing returns?*

If the answer was yes—meaning the blood, sweat, and frustration weren't remotely paying off—he'd follow up with another classic: "Go where the sun shines the hottest." To me, this means directing my attention to where the energy, action, and opportunity is, as opposed to just going through the motions, eking out crumbs out of obligation.

Dad's wisdom is a potent reminder: Don't stay stuck in old, ineffectual rhythms because they feel safe. Trust that what's meant for you doesn't require you to drain your life force to experience success or fulfillment.

Never one to sugarcoat or side-shimmy his way around what he observed, Dad would call me out if he caught me being hypocritical. Especially when I was a fountain of good advice to others but avoided applying that very same advice to my own life. Like if he saw me blowing off my own doctors' visits, he'd say, "Practice what you preach."

I'll never forget the day I was booked to appear on *The Oprah Winfrey Show*. I called my parents to share the exciting news. Naturally, they were overjoyed for me. But Dad slid in one little piece of wisdom before we hung up: "stay humble." Later, at his celebration-of-life service, I learned that when the episode aired, he ditched the business conference he was attending so he and a few work buddies could huddle around the TV in his hotel room, cheering me on, with a box of tissues at the ready.

He'd remind me, "Keep the promises you make to yourself, because time is precious." If we can't keep the promises we make to ourselves, how are we going to keep those we make to others (at least without generating unneeded resentment)? Watching him keep his biggest promise, to get to know himself more before he died, inspired me to do the same. I hope it inspires you, too.

My favorite nugget of guidance from Dad came toward the end, when he told me to "stop and smell the lizards." He meant "roses," but his medications had scrambled the metaphors. In fact, he kept talking about the "lizards" as if they were my cautionary tale. Like him, I am most at ease when I have a job to do. But if I didn't check my tendencies, I'd forget to smell the lizards, too.

These days those little reptiles are my north star. A simple reminder to be more conscious and intentional about where I put my energy. And though my heart is heavy, I look up at the stars and down at the lizards and say, "Yes." Yes to breathing. Yes to taking care of myself. Yes to allowing the ruptures to rearrange me, instead of dodging and weaving past them as fast as possible, missing a whole lot of gems along the way. Yes to life.

More than three years after my dad died, I can say that I am starting to feel better. Not because I have everything figured out or my heart is fully mended (it never will be) but because I'm more at ease with life's natural ebbs and flows, more willing to breathe through whatever emotions come up on any given day, and more confident in my ability to weather the inevitable storms. So, yes, life fell apart, and that long and winding road somehow brought me back home to myself.

BOTH/AND

After living in upstate New York for 17 years, Brian and I decided to sell the home we built and relocate to Connecticut—20 minutes from my mom. It was a bittersweet change, but not because we were sad to leave the Catskills. We weren't. For years, we'd been dreaming about the house we eventually bought. Long before we moved in, we sat and visualized it together, making lists of all the exciting elements it would contain—like a two-car garage and ample closet space. We knew what it would look like, feel like, and be like because we had pictured it in our mind's eye so many times. Together, we kept watering that seedling vision until our hopes became our reality.

To say we're happy is an understatement. We *love* our new house and town. I've seen more wildlife in the last three weeks than in all my years living in the rural mountains (including black bear, pheasant, foxes, and one wily bobcat, which I saw stalking toward me at 5:30 A.M. when I was out walking the dogs in my bare feet and underwear).

And yet Dad isn't here to enjoy this new chapter with us, and that's painful. I think of him when I cook on Sundays and how he would have held court around my kitchen island. I can picture him reading the paper by the fire or helping Brian at the grill. He would have loved it here—especially the paved driveway. Asphalt was his love language, after all.

In some ways, coming home to the area he and my mom lived in for over 30 years makes me feel closer to him. I remember him in the restaurants, stores, flea market, walks, drives, and all the other nooks and crannies we used to inhabit together. He shows up in my thoughts and memories and the occasional spot-on sign.

I love this, and it guts me.

I'm excited about this next chapter, and I'm depressed.

I'm grateful, and I'm grieving.

I'm energized, and I'm exhausted.

I feel closer to Dad and yet so far away.

I call this surreal duality the *both/and* place. The joyful moments always have a tinge of sadness; the higher the high, the more prominent the awareness of my loss.

Coming to grips with this is important because this *both/and* feeling never goes away. For example, it was thrilling to finish the first draft of this book. Then came the sadness as I remembered that I couldn't call and tell him about it.

But maybe the *both/and* is a more normal and realistic place—truer to a dynamic, three-dimensional life.

I'm healthy, *and* I have cancer.

I'm a life-loving person, *and* I have a lot of anxiety.

I'm bighearted *and* closed off.

I'm successful *and* unsuccessful (at a whole lot of things). *Both/and.*

Sometimes it's hard to fathom how we can hold opposite feelings and realities at the same time, but two things can be true at once, and our hearts are wise enough to hold the contradiction.

In the months (and years) after Dad died, I felt guilty for even allowing myself to feel positive. Though parts of my life were awesome, it felt wrong to acknowledge anything other than the awful experience of Dad's physical absence. Staying in the pain made me feel like I was staying connected to him. I wanted to be like those Italian ladies who wear long black dresses for the rest of their lives, because I unconsciously equated being happy with abandoning Dad.

But the more space I gave myself to explore the subterranean world of emotions inside me, the more capable I was of embracing and holding the duality. The grief train *and* the celebrations.

Joy isn't exclusive to the good times; it can exist in the hard times, too. I learned this with my own diagnosis. In the beginning, getting sick helped me recalibrate—and that felt really good and useful. I learned how to take care of myself for the first time, and as I've shared, the results paid off. Though I was technically sick, I'd never felt better.

My wake-up call woke up other parts of me, too. Parts that had also craved healing. But after a while, it was easy to go back to sleep. To slip into old, hardwired, comfortable patterns of being and relating, because they were familiar.

I used to beat myself up about not staying in a perpetual state of awakeness, as if *not* living my life "like every day was my last" meant that I was lazy, ungrateful, or worse—willfully blowing off the hard-won wisdom I'd learned in the cancer trenches. Maybe you can relate in your own way.

Of course, none of that is true. It's why I often come back to Jung's notion of orbiting. The idea that we circle around the same themes our entire lives. And with each passing orbit, we reach the next circle of meaning (understanding, integration, assimilation). Translation: it's normal to step in the same shit again and again, each time with a new willingness to go deeper. What a relief!

If you find yourself orbiting, please don't beat yourself up, mistakenly believing you're in a downward spiral of stuckness. Believe me, I know the temptation, but orbiting truly is the instrument of our healing. We cycle through change, and all the feelings that come with it. And with each trip around the sun, our souls get wiser, our hearts expand, and we orbit to a new layer of ourselves in and among the *both/and*.

TAKE IT ONE STEP AT A TIME (NOT ONE DAY AT A TIME)

One day at a time can be *a lot*. One step at a time helps you digest and steady yourself. It's gentler on the nervous system. Some moments will be tough (I've certainly shared a few of my doozies). Others will feel softer. If you're prone to sky-high expectations of yourself, lower the bar. In fact, put it so damn low you could trip over it.

Imagine you've just come out of a major surgery. Would you expect yourself to have the mental and physical ability to just get back to life as usual? Hopefully not. Hopefully, you'd be willing to allow your body time to recuperate. Remember that loss, traumatic events, and unexpected shit pickles (even those that are for the best) are draining in ways you may not even be aware of.

As you learn how to navigate this stage of your orbit, be patient with yourself, dear one. You are not a machine. Taking things one step at a time allows you to set limits on how much you can handle in any given moment. For me, after Dad died, my bandwidth for "normal" life was next to nothing. I literally thought there was something wrong with me as I struggled to get out of bed.

I don't recognize myself anymore, I'd think. The things that lit me up previously felt dry and unappealing—like stale saltines.

Why can't I remember anything? Basic word recall went out the window. (Grief brain will do that to you.) The day I couldn't remember the word for cat—"you know, the animal that says meow"—I nearly scheduled a brain MRI. *Great, now I have tumors in my noggin, too—just what I need.*

Then I remembered: this is what the process of repair looks like.

It may even feel like your body and spirit are totally (and endlessly) rearranging themselves. *Does this still fit? Do I even like this anymore? Is this worn-out woobie ready to be retired?*

As with any major reorg, you will need breaks, hugs, and space. Do yourself a solid and allow them.

Taking one step at a time is true for relationships, too—especially when there's tension as a result of changing roles or family dynamics. In that case, don't expect things to be repaired right away. Loss brings up a lot of unresolved issues for *everyone*, not just you.

Finding resolution takes a minute (or a lifetime), and let's be honest, relationships don't always work out the way we wish. That can certainly be painful—another cause for grief. But just because we don't get the relationship we wanted doesn't always mean things haven't worked out in the spiritual sense. On some level, everything does. For those uncomfortable in-between moments, it can help to remember Rumi's wisdom: "Out beyond ideas of wrongdoing and rightdoing, there is a field. I'll meet you there."

After going through this journey with my chosen father, I have a different kind of peace with my biological father and the role he played in my life. As a result of exploring and healing aspects of my own trauma, I have more compassion for the adversity BD faced in his life, too. I forgive him for the pain he caused, and I'm sorry for how I wounded him. Though he wasn't meant to be my day-to-day dad, I'm grateful he was part of making me and that I have some of the best parts of his nature.

Like it or not, no physical relationship is perfect or forever. And perhaps no relationship solely exists in physical form. Nevertheless, our bonds remain. Maybe when we shed our bodies, our baggage goes with them. Suddenly it's "only love," like one big, free-spirited Burning Man Festival in the sky (without the dust, sweat, and hangovers). Wouldn't that be a gas? I guess we'll see one day.

LOOK FOR THE LIGHT

One of my grandma's favorite mottoes was "Don't curse the darkness, light a candle."

When it *all* feels like too much, look for the light. Life is full of ups and downs, especially when we're committed to living it fully. But no matter how dark it gets, there's always light to be found—small moments that remind us that beauty still exists. A child's laughter, sun on our face, positive memories of the people we've lost. And, of course, a wagging tail. These are the things that point us toward the nourishing light.

For me, the creative process is how I find the light. That's what writing this book was all about. Using my pen to turn my pain into purpose. In fact, when I started this process, I set two intentions—one for you and one for me.

"May this book help to normalize conversations around difficult emotions so that people feel less alone and crazy. And may I heal deeper parts of myself as a result of this writing."

That goes for both what I've learned and for the passing on of my dad's wisdom. In fact, his light lives on in my heart, these pages, and maybe even in you.

And here's the thing, we're all creative—especially the folks who think they're not. In fact, we use creativity in everything we do, each and every day. Figuring out how to patch a leaky faucet? Creative. Finding a new doctor? Creative. Fixing your teeth after life kicked you in the choppers? Very creative.

See, you're practically Picasso already. So, if you have a flicker of creative fire burning inside you, stoke it. Don't worry if you don't know what you're doing. None of us know *anything* when we're first starting out. In my experience, we learn by *doing*. Stay curious and you'll figure it out, I promise.

Regardless of what avenue you choose, light is all around you, even on the darkest days.

CULTIVATE JOY

If life has brought you to your knees and atrophied your joy muscles, you may be thinking, *How am I supposed to find joy at a time like this?* It hardly seems like perfect conditions to have a blast. *Everything I've loved and held dear is evaporating before my eyes. Let's party!*

I get it. I really do.

In the early days of my grief the thought of cultivating joy seemed impossible, infuriating, and worse—insulting. It was *all* those things and more, which is why I had to fight for it, and you might, too.

And yet, joy is essential to healing. It also keeps you from becoming the type of person who writes Facebook screeds with no paragraph returns or texts in ALL CAPS.

Here's why this is important: Joy isn't just a feel-good emotion. Joy is medicine. It affects our biology at the cellular level and is a key indicator for our overall well-being. Joy boosts our resilience, making us better able to cope with life's ups, downs, and crashes. It helps reduce anxiety and depression. Joy helps us sleep better. It even lowers blood pressure and improves cardiovascular health. Basically, joy is like a natural health booster and painkiller, with zero side effects.

Part of my own heart mending has come from the joy of connecting with other people on the same path of healing I am on. I used to pride myself on being a lone wolf, handling life on my own with self-reliance and determination. But these last few years have taught me that I need to get out of my hermit cave and sweats and back into my relationships with my crew. We're not meant to do life alone. We're meant to celebrate together, witness each other, participate in rituals, and share our stories—the good and the bad. The downright hilarious and the hideous.

Look, I know that joy will never replace what you or I have lost. It's not meant to. But depriving ourselves of it is the opposite of what we need when we're struggling. In fact, the more we're struggling, the *more* we need to prioritize joy.

Much of our recovery takes place through the process of changing our thoughts and adjusting our behavior. We can't control what happened, but we can control how we respond. We can choose to proactively find and fight for joy, even in the midst of hardship.

George Bonanno, professor of clinical psychology at Columbia University, describes grief as an emotion that oscillates: "Over time the cycle widens, and gradually we return to a state of equilibrium. One of the ways we achieve this adaptive oscillation in and out of sadness is by switching to more positive states of mind." He goes on to say that most of us are more capable of making the switch than we think. "We don't expect to find joy and even laughter within our pain, but when we do, it makes sense, and we feel better, even if temporarily."

One of the reasons I've included humor in this book is because laughter helps us absorb and metabolize the medicine. Personally speaking, humor keeps me sane and, you guessed it, joyful. I need to poke fun at cancer, grief, death, and, most of all, myself. When I'm at my lowest, I look for something to laugh about. If I can't find anything, I create it.

MORE LIKE THIS

Many of the seeds planted throughout this book are meant to help us connect more deeply to ourselves and to what matters most in our lives. Whatever crossroads we find ourselves at, this level of self-connection will eventually build self-trust. And when that muscle of self-trust is strengthened, weathering uncertainty becomes less daunting.

Yes, we may struggle and stumble again, but damned if we don't know how to get back up. Think back on who you were a few years ago and all that you've navigated since. There were plenty of unknowns then (some of them unthinkable) and yet you managed to get here, to this place of wanting to heal and experience deeper authenticity. Hey, that's something to be very proud of. Let your past survival be your prologue to thriving.

Remember the post-traumatic growth we talked about in Chapter 5? Well, this is an important concept to keep in mind as you move ahead, with bravery, into your new life. You don't have to wait for all the pieces to fall perfectly into place to start living more fully, or for the first time, or even again. It's OK to rebuild, armed with the priceless insight you had to develop to survive—hard-won wisdom no one would ever choose to earn but which makes you more real and experienced for it.

In different ways, we have all become more ourselves, and that's a beautiful thing.

You are and will always be a survivor. It's OK to thrive once more. It's OK to let go of old ways that no longer serve the person you've become—scars and all. Dad's diagnosis, and subsequent death, woke me up. I'd trade all the awareness I've fought for, and any of the "positives," if I could only go back to the way things were when he was here and we were us. No amount of personal growth is worth his loss. But the universe keeps expanding, slowing for no one.

My new mantra: *Don't go back to sleep.*

Before we conclude our time together, I want to go back to Martha's Vineyard with you. To that special restaurant with the magnificent view of the ocean and that profound and deeply moving advice my father gave me that I wasn't ready to think about: "You know, love, I wish I had given myself more time like this. Your golden years aren't promised. Figure out what your 'more time like this' looks like, and do it now. Make now your golden years."

More big medicine to me from my amazing pops. And now I'm passing it on to you. Figure out your "more time like this" and make your life golden, my friend.

Hold fast to the courage needed to let *all* of yourself be loved—that's the lesson I've learned time and time again from my many ruptures. Don't avoid the parts of yourself that ask for the most tenderness. The so-called ugly parts that need to be witnessed and held. Like it or not, we're all complicated beings who share one common thread: a need to love and be loved.

Loving ourselves and others through the good times and devastating times is what life is all about. In fact, there's no greater success to achieve. Ultimately, love not only showed me how to grieve—it showed me how to live.

Love allowed me to thaw my stuck feelings and live more wholeheartedly.

Love gave me the courage to be free—not free from the pain but free from the *fear* of pain and the barrier it creates to love.

Love eventually allowed me to provide for myself exactly what my father had given me every second I was lucky enough to have him in my life: the feelings of being lovable, safe, and good enough.

This is the journey of our humanness. To connect to love, our true power, in order to heal the wounds that keep us stuck. It's a simple, jagged path with no easy pass or mileage points. But all roads lead there—even the ones that take us off track.

Thank you for walking this path with me.

Now, keep going. And remember to smell the fragrant lizards along the way.

ACKNOWLEDGMENTS

To Pamela Cannon, my brilliant editor. Without you this book wouldn't exist. Thank you for your unwavering enthusiasm, can-do spirit, and "ok, now you're just showing off" candor. For crawling into the trenches with me (index cards and all), and for every edit that made this book something I am very proud of. I appreciate you and your very big heart, my friend.

To Suzanne Guillette, thank you for pouring your poetry onto these pages with me. For pushing me to go deeper, and for showing me ways to express the inexpressible. Your guidance not only made this book richer, it helped me grow.

To Patty Gift, thank you for championing a topic most shy away from. For giving me the space and grace to take my time, find my way, and create my music. *Je t'adore, lion.*

To Reid Tracy, thank you for saying yes to my writing so long ago (even the cuss words). Your friendship means the world, moon, and stars to me.

To Melody Guy, thank you for coaxing out even more magic. For finding the nooks and crannies that needed more heart (or clearer explanation!), and for allowing me to go to places I was afraid to go to. Once there, you said, "It's OK. That's normal. Keep going."

To my wonderful literary agents, Scott Hoffman and Steve Troha, thank you for believing in my work and welcoming me into the Folio fold.

To Sarah Hall, Krystin White (Cookie), Lindsay McGinty, and Lizzi Marshall, thank you for helping me spread this book far and wide.

To my amazing team: Mandi, Hayley, Deidra, Abby, Morgan, Cameron, Justin, John, thank you for your creative hearts, big smarts, and caring spirits. And for loving sandwiches as much as I do. But extra thanks to Mandi Rivieccio, our Chief Creative Officer, for being a tender titan and my favorite person to word chef with.

To my Inner Circle Wellness community and Thrive Mastermind members, thank you for your desire to learn and grow alongside me.

To Carol, thank you for guiding me through so many storms.

To Jeanette, thank you for giving me a book on grief. It scared me at first. And then it kicked off a healing I didn't know possible.

To my dearest True Blues: Nick, Terri, Regena, Gabby, Dani, Rachel, Kate, Gina, John R, Kristen, and Bill, thank you for your beautiful friendship on my best and worst days.

To my best friend, Marie Forleo, thank you for bunny cups, dream clubs, psychics follies, ambulance emojis, endless laughter, and the safest place for ugly cries.

To my beloved husband, Brian Fassett, thank you for helping me cull my compound sentences, and for saying things like "less Chekhov play, more Hemingway" (even though I still don't know what that means). But most of all, thank you for loving me and this fantastic life we've built together. And thank you for loving Dad with such generosity.

To my incredible mom, Aura Carr, thank you for being a constant source of love and support throughout my life. Your courage in difficult times has taught me how to face my own challenges with fierce grace, while your exuberant curiosity for life reminds me to cultivate my own seeker's spirit. I am forever grateful for your unwavering presence and inspiration.

And most of all, thank you, Dad . . .

ABOUT
THE AUTHOR

KRIS CARR is a multiple *New York Times* best-selling author, wellness activist, and cancer thriver.

She's been called a "force of nature" by *O, the Oprah Magazine* and was named a "new role model" by the *The New York Times*. Kris is also a member of Oprah's Super Soul 100, which recognizes the most influential thought leaders today. Other media appearances include *Glamour*, *Prevention*, *Scientific American*, *Good Morning America*, the *Today* show, *Forbes*, the *Wall Street Journal*, and *The Oprah Winfrey Show*. Kris has helped millions of people take charge of their health and live like they mean it through her award-winning blog, books, online courses, and membership communities. You can find her at kriscarr.com.